First World War
and Army of Occupation
War Diary
France, Belgium and Germany

25 DIVISION
75 Infantry Brigade
Prince of Wales's Volunteers (South Lancashire Regiment)
8th Battalion
26 September 1915 - 31 January 1918

WO95/2250/3

The Naval & Military Press Ltd
www.nmarchive.com
Published in association with The National Archives

Published by

The Naval & Military Press Ltd

Unit 10 Ridgewood Industrial Park,

Uckfield, East Sussex,

TN22 5QE England

Tel: +44 (0) 1825 749494

www.naval-military-press.com

www.nmarchive.com

This diary has been reprinted in facsimile from the original. Any imperfections are inevitably reproduced and the quality may fall short of modern type and cartographic standards.

© **Crown Copyright**
Images reproduced by permission of The National Archives, London, England, 2015.

Contents

Document type	Place/Title	Date From	Date To
Heading	8th Bn Sth Lancs Regt. Sep 1915-Jan 1918		
Heading	25th Division 75th Bde 8th S. Lancashire Regt. Vol I Sept & Oct 15		
Miscellaneous	To D.A.G. 3rd Echelon Base.		
War Diary	Aldershot	26/09/1915	26/09/1915
War Diary	Boulogne	27/09/1915	28/09/1915
War Diary	Strazeele	28/09/1915	28/09/1915
War Diary	Bailleul	29/09/1915	29/09/1915
War Diary	Hants Farm (Ploegsteert)	03/10/1915	03/10/1915
War Diary	Fire Trenches (Ploegsteert Wood)	07/10/1915	12/10/1915
War Diary	Ploegsteert Wood	13/10/1915	30/10/1915
Heading	25th Division 75 Bde 8th S. Lancs Vol 2		
War Diary	Ploegsteert Wood	01/11/1915	03/11/1915
War Diary	Moat Farm	04/11/1915	12/11/1915
War Diary	Ploegsteert Wood (Trenches)	16/11/1915	16/11/1915
War Diary	Moat Farm	18/11/1915	30/11/1915
Heading	25th Div 8th S. Lancs Vol 3		
War Diary	Moat Farm (Ploegsteert)	01/12/1915	31/12/1915
Heading	8th Battn. South Lancashire Regiment. January 1916		
War Diary	Geslues Farm (Ploegsteert)	01/01/1916	29/01/1916
War Diary	Courtecourt	30/01/1916	31/01/1916
Heading	8th Battn. South Lancashire Regiment. February 1916		
Heading	8th S. Lancs Vol 5		
War Diary	Courtecourt	01/02/1916	29/02/1916
Heading	8th Battn. South Lancashire Regiment. March 1916		
Heading	8 S. Lancs Vol 6		
War Diary	Courte	01/03/1916	01/03/1916
War Diary	Courte Croix Divisnl Rest	02/03/1916	04/03/1916
War Diary	Billets	05/03/1916	09/03/1916
War Diary	Thiennes	10/03/1916	10/03/1916
War Diary	Ammattes	11/03/1916	14/03/1916
War Diary	Hestrus	15/03/1916	17/03/1916
War Diary	Marquay	18/03/1916	31/03/1916
Heading	8th Battn. South Lancashire Regiment. April 1916		
War Diary	Marquay	01/04/1916	20/04/1916
War Diary	Ecoivre	21/04/1916	27/04/1916
War Diary	O.61 to a 62	28/04/1916	29/04/1916
War Diary	O. 60 to O.62	29/04/1916	30/04/1916
Heading	8th Battn. South Lancashire Regiment. May 1916		
War Diary	Neuville St Vasst O.60 to O.62	01/05/1916	01/05/1916
War Diary	Trenches	02/05/1916	04/05/1916
War Diary	Neuville St Vasst	05/05/1916	10/05/1916
War Diary	Trenches	11/05/1916	16/05/1916
War Diary	Ecoivres	17/05/1916	20/05/1916
War Diary	Trenches	20/05/1916	24/05/1916
War Diary	Neuville St Vasst	25/05/1916	31/05/1916
Heading	8th Battn. South Lancashire Regiment. June 1916		
War Diary	Berneuil	19/06/1916	24/06/1916
War Diary	Talmas	25/06/1916	27/06/1916
War Diary	Toutencourt	28/06/1916	30/06/1916

War Diary	Neuville St Vasst	01/06/1916	01/06/1916
War Diary	Acq	02/06/1916	02/06/1916
War Diary	Bethonsart	03/06/1916	14/06/1916
War Diary	Averdoingt		
War Diary	Fortel		
War Diary	Beaumetz		
Heading	8th Battalion South Lancashire Regiment. July 1916		
War Diary	Hedauville	02/07/1916	07/07/1916
War Diary	Ovillers	08/07/1916	16/07/1916
War Diary	Senlis	17/07/1917	17/07/1917
War Diary	Amplier	18/07/1916	21/07/1916
War Diary	Louvencourt	22/07/1916	22/07/1916
War Diary	Acheux	23/07/1916	23/07/1916
War Diary	Auchonvillers & Trenches	25/07/1916	31/07/1916
Miscellaneous	Messages And Signals.	04/07/1916	04/07/1916
Heading	1/8th Battalion South Lancashire Regiment August 1916		
War Diary	Beaumont Hamel	30/07/1916	25/08/1916
War Diary	Forceville	25/08/1916	25/08/1916
War Diary	Authueille	26/08/1916	26/08/1916
War Diary	Leipsic Salient	27/08/1916	31/08/1916
Heading	8th. South Lancs Regt. September 1916		
War Diary	Leipsic Redoubt	01/09/1916	30/09/1916
Heading	8th Battn. South Lancashire Regiment. October 1916		
War Diary	Zollern Redoubt	01/10/1916	01/10/1916
War Diary	Hessian Trench	03/10/1916	23/10/1916
War Diary	Hem	24/10/1916	31/10/1916
Heading	8th Battn. South Lancashire Regiment. November 1916		
War Diary	Schaexken Bailleul	01/11/1916	30/11/1916
Heading	8th Battn. South Lancashire Regiment. December 1916		
War Diary	Ploegsteert	02/12/1916	31/12/1916
War Diary	Romarin	31/12/1916	31/12/1916
War Diary	De Seule	02/01/1917	31/01/1917
War Diary	In The Field	01/02/1917	26/02/1917
War Diary	Eecke	01/03/1917	11/03/1917
War Diary	Wardrecques	12/03/1917	13/03/1917
War Diary	Quercamp	14/03/1917	19/03/1917
War Diary	Zudausques	20/03/1917	20/03/1917
War Diary	Lynde	21/03/1917	21/03/1917
War Diary	Le Petit	22/03/1917	22/03/1917
War Diary	Sec Bois	23/03/1917	31/03/1917
War Diary	Outtersteene	01/04/1917	03/04/1917
War Diary	Neuve Eglise	05/04/1917	12/04/1917
War Diary	Bulford Camp	13/04/1917	18/04/1917
War Diary	Jesus Camp	19/04/1917	21/04/1917
War Diary	Strazeele	22/04/1917	22/04/1917
War Diary	St. Marie	23/04/1917	23/04/1917
War Diary	Cappel	24/04/1917	30/04/1917
Heading	May to July 1917 8th S. Lancs. Regt.		
War Diary	Outtersteene	01/05/1917	09/05/1917
War Diary	Steenwerck	10/05/1917	15/05/1917
War Diary	La Creche	15/05/1917	28/05/1917
War Diary	Ravelsburg	29/05/1917	31/05/1917
War Diary	Neuveeglise	01/06/1917	06/06/1917
War Diary	Wulverghem	06/06/1917	08/06/1917
War Diary	Neuveeglise	09/06/1917	28/06/1917

War Diary	Beaumetz Les Aire	28/06/1917	30/06/1917
Miscellaneous	8th Battalion South Lancs Regiment Report On Operations 6th/10th June 1917		
War Diary	Beaumetz les Aire	01/07/1917	30/07/1917
War Diary	Westhoek Ridge	01/08/1917	06/08/1917
War Diary	Ypres	07/08/1917	07/08/1917
War Diary	Railway Wood	08/08/1917	08/08/1917
War Diary	Halifax Camp	09/08/1917	10/08/1917
War Diary	Westhoek Ridge	11/08/1917	13/08/1917
War Diary	Dominion Camp	14/08/1917	15/08/1917
War Diary	Ypres	16/08/1917	17/08/1917
War Diary	Eecke Area	18/08/1917	19/08/1917
War Diary	Steenvoorde Area	25/08/1917	01/09/1917
War Diary	Devonshire Camp	02/09/1917	02/09/1917
War Diary	Dickebusch Area	03/09/1917	05/09/1917
War Diary	Zillebeke Bund	06/09/1917	09/09/1917
War Diary	Canal Reserve Camp	15/09/1917	15/09/1917
War Diary	Halifax Camp	11/09/1917	12/09/1917
War Diary	Caestre Area	13/09/1917	13/09/1917
War Diary	Steenbecque Area	14/09/1917	14/09/1917
War Diary	Allouagne Area	15/09/1917	27/09/1917
War Diary	Cite St Pierre	28/09/1917	28/09/1917
War Diary	Lens	29/09/1917	30/09/1917
War Diary	Lens Sector	01/10/1917	04/10/1917
War Diary	Bully Grenay Area	05/10/1917	05/10/1917
War Diary	Houchin Area	06/10/1917	06/10/1917
War Diary	Le Preol	07/10/1917	12/10/1917
War Diary	Canal Left Sector	13/10/1917	31/10/1917
War Diary	Le Preol	01/11/1917	04/11/1917
War Diary	Canal Sector	05/11/1917	23/11/1917
War Diary	Le Preol	24/11/1917	28/11/1917
War Diary	Fouquereuil	29/11/1917	29/11/1917
War Diary	Burbure	30/11/1917	30/11/1917
War Diary	Beaumetz Lez Aire	01/12/1917	03/12/1917
War Diary	Gomiecourt Camp	04/12/1917	05/12/1917
War Diary	Rocquigny	06/12/1917	09/12/1917
War Diary	Monmouth Camp Bapaume	10/12/1917	15/12/1917
War Diary	No 5 Camp Favreuil	16/12/1917	21/12/1917
War Diary	Lagnicourt Sector	22/12/1917	31/12/1917
War Diary	Lagnicourt Left Sub Sector	01/01/1918	02/01/1918
War Diary	Favreuil	03/01/1918	14/01/1918
War Diary	Lagnicourt Left Sub Sector	15/01/1918	20/01/1918
War Diary	Vaulx	21/01/1918	26/01/1918
War Diary	Favreuil	27/01/1918	31/01/1918
Miscellaneous	This Document WO95/2250		

25TH DIVISION
75TH INFY BDE

8TH BN STH LANCS REGT.
SEP 1915-JAN 1918

(DISBANDED 6 FEB 1918)

121/7431

25th Division

75 Bde

8th L Lancashire Regt.
Vol. I

Sep 1 & Oct 15

To.
D.A.G.
3rd Echelon Base —

Forwarded for Information

A.G.N. Lang Lt Colonel
Commanding 8th S. Lancs Regt.

Army Form C. 2118

WAR DIARY
or
INTELLIGENCE SUMMARY
(Erase heading not required.)

Instructions regarding War Diaries and Intelligence Summaries are contained in F.S. Regs., Part II. and the Staff Manual respectively. Title Pages will be prepared in manuscript.

September & October 1915

Place	Date	Hour	Summary of Events and Information	Remarks and references to Appendices
Aldershot	26/9/15	6.45 P.M. 7 P.M.	Left Govt School in 2 trains. Details & transport left 2.5" & 10.25 PM & went via Southampton. Strength of Battn 30 officers 920 other ranks.	
Boulogne	27/9/15	12.30 A.M.	Disembarked, marched to Rest Camp (Ostrohove) 3 miles off.	
—	28/9/15	5.10 P.M.	Left for Pont de Briques station. Arrived Strazeele 2.15 P.M.	
Strazeele	—	8.30 P.M.	Arrd & went into billets. Rained steadily from 5 P.M.	
Bailleul	29/9/15	4.30 P.M.	Arrived town & into billets. Whole Battn in Rue de la Gare. Rained all day.	
Hauts (Ploegsteert)	3/10/15	6 P.M.	and & relieved the 16th Canadians. In Reserve to XI Cheshires. Enemy's machine guns active firing on La Creche road, south of this farm. On 6th inst their big guns so well as machine guns very active firing all round the farm "TOUQUET BERTHE" & Bn HQrs. We lost 2/Lt d'Beauchamp & No 15000 Sergt Holden – Machine Gun Officer & Sergt by the premature explosion of a bomb while instructing a class of officers.	
Fir Trees (Ploegsteert Wood)	9/10/15	2.18" 6 P.M. 11 P.M. 12 m" 3 P.M.	"HQrs & Capt H. ONeil (our Battn M.O.) killed wounded by a rifle grenade in front trenches. Relieved 11th Cheshires & went into B Coy Reserve. Enemy fired on our aeroplane. Conditions normal. Pte W. Hayward Killed on lookout duty in the firing trench by an enemy sniper.	

1875 Wt. W593/826 1,000,000 4/15 J.B.C. & A. A.D.S.S./Forms/C. 2118.

Army Form C. 2118

WAR DIARY
or
INTELLIGENCE SUMMARY
(Erase heading not required.)

October 1915

Instructions regarding War Diaries and Intelligence Summaries are contained in F.S. Regs., Part II. and the Staff Manual respectively. Title Pages will be prepared in manuscript.

Place	Date	Hour	Summary of Events and Information	Remarks and references to Appendices
Ploegsteert Wood	13/10/15	2 P.M.	Our Artillery – 25th Div. – made demonstration against the Enemy in front of the line till 4 P.M. After that there was occasional artillery fire on both sides. No damage done whatever along our Bde. front.	
—	15/10/15	6 P.M.	Relieved by 5th Bde. Reserve. – Relieved in trenches by XI Cheshires. No 15786 Corpl. Pritchard "C" Coy'y wounded while asleep in tent (by unaimed fire).	
—	18/10/15	4-5 P.M.	Enemy fired about 20 large H.E. Shells which fell around TOUQUET BERTHE Farm during the afternoon. Shrapnel was also fired causing the following casualties. No 15399 Pte J. Parrott "C" Coy (who died on 19th inst.) & 15597 Pte W. McCormack "C" Coy.	
—	19/10/15		No 15236 Pte R. Pape "C" Coy wounded in foot by a stray bullet.	
—	21/10/15	6 P.M.	Relieved XI Cheshires in trenches. — Rain during night.	
—	25/10/15		Very much wetter weather while in Reserve. Relieved in trenches (fire) by Cheshires. Weather again into trenches.	
—	29/10/15 30/10/15		Weather wet, in the trenches, two trenches, support trenches in bad condition, repairing, a feathered spark in them. Enemy not active in our front.	

J.M.
2.11.15

25th Hussein St S Lanes
Vol: 2

75" Rob

121/7656

Nov. 15

WAR DIARY
or
INTELLIGENCE SUMMARY

Army Form C. 2118

NOVEMBER 1915

Place	Date	Hour	Summary of Events and Information	Remarks and references to Appendices
Ploegsteert Wood.	1st 2nd 3rd		Rained off & on all day & night. All available new armies repairing parapets & drains. Largements of fire trench. Some work also done in support trenches. Right Half Bn. Support trenches (114-116) in a very bad state. Working parties also out strengthening these in rear of trenches. Snow shower during day. Other Bn. Coyd working in fire trenches. 3 Casualties. 13768 Pte. E. Ferguson killed by fragment of whizzbang. 14425 - G. Smith wounded by bullet. Died in course of evening. J. Sharpe wounded. 15344 - S. Smalley (Sniper) wounded in head & built. Died shortly afterwards.	R. St. Coll. 113-116 Cutterside dy 117-118 d.s.d. T.W. 119-120 S.Tr.Sp.
	4th		14744 L/c J. Horsfall killed. Shot through head. Reserve a unit in XI Cheshires. New Batt. H.Q.	
Mont Farm	8th		1 Casualty. 14643 Pte. L. Davis. Killed by shell in Ploegsteert.	
	10th		2 Casualties. 15246 Pte. R. Smith wounded standing to in time. XI Cheshire Artillery a little more active in trenches. Shrapnel during midday. 14010 Corporal W.B. Allen wounded accidentally. 14351 Pte. J.A. Thomas.	
	11th		Weather while in trenches v. cold, frost at night. Worked pumping water out of trenches & building up parapets which	

WAR DIARY
or
INTELLIGENCE SUMMARY

(Erase heading not required.)

Army Form C.

November 1915

Place	Date	Hour	Summary of Events and Information	Remarks reference Appendices
MOEG-steert Wood (Trenches)	16th		Kept a listening post in place. Trench 119 untenable in consequence. Fatr. heart. Enemy thrown a shell into Coy. Emplacement . Artillery on both sides helped to stamp up on. Continuous bombardment of the enemy trenches during the afternoon bombarded the enemy trench line.	*LE GHEER
MOAT FARM	18th		1st Cheshires relieved us in the trenches in the afternoon. When on a working party the following the de Ghier the following Casualties occurred 14572. Pte J.A. Vile (killed) 15325 Pte A. Lockett (wounded) 17010 Pte H. Goodacre (wounded) and on	
	19th 20th 22nd		14300 Pte M.A. Morrissey (wounded + died from same Shell offerwards) Cpl G. Dettli Telegraph adjutant (gass) + Cpl R. Prior + one other C. Company Relieved XI Cheshires in trenches. Weather misty + wet.	
	24th		dull & cos. Weather fine misty + wet pte Enemy's artillery doing a lot of work to retain + have ften hindered 17145 Pte J. Clark 15116 Pte R. Swain wounded also 16694 Pte W.D. Sanders, 14714 Pte R. Matthews	
	26th		by Sharpnel. also 16694 Pte W.D. Sanders who died late in day. + 17066 L/Cpl J.W.B. Parr who died late in day. No 13985 L/Cpl J. Nuttall killed by Whizzbang Shots throughout the day. Jans Wheat	
	27th 30th			

J.A.G.R. Laughnel
Capt. 8th R. Lancs

Sh. L. Lanes.
Vol: 3

Miss Russell
3ᴬ

D/
7936

25 H/5/12

2Cc/

Army Form C. 2118

WAR DIARY or INTELLIGENCE SUMMARY
(Erase heading not required.)

December 1915

Strength 1st Dec 1915 Officers 29. O. Ranks 892

Place	Date	Hour	Summary of Events and Information	Remarks and references to Appendices
MONT FARM (PLOEGST-EERT)	1st		In Reserve Billets. Operations No. 10 took place A.M. & P.M.	
	2nd		Relieved XI Cheshires in Trenches. Enemy mortar active. Then usual desultory fire. Fired a mine was exploded in front Trench 99 — after which things became normal. Nothing unusual.	
	3rd	10 – 2 p.m.		
	4th		About 3.30 – 4 p.m. Enemy Aeroplane from S.E. reconnoitred our trenches at each corner — enemy withdrew. 107.324. Pte J. Briggs (Sniper) Signaller wounded by bullet. 107,216 Pte L. Sherman wounded by bullet.	
	5th			
	6th			
	7th		Relieved by XI Cheshires and returned to Billets.	
	8th		Enemy aeroplane over Ploegsteert. Altogether 29 Shells dropped. Two dropped hit 6 or 7 other houses who were in the building, slightly wounded as some and frightfully occupied by "D" Coy Signallers. Station of the 4 position of the together. Shelling commenced about 12.15 and finished 12.45 p.m.	
	9th		Shells on barns between eleven windows & 4 position of the together. Shelling commenced about 12.15 and finished 12.45 p.m.	
	11th		Enemy dropped 3 H.E. Shells within about 50 yards of St George's farm in damage done. shrapnel shells & Hummas bombs from English trenches on Stafford Posts to "B" Coy. Sgt Hughes Second Aeroplanes hovering over — Three of our own to bring down one of them. This above 11 am.	
	12th		Wither was lovely. Saturday evening. Lt Hammond to get clear, this above 11 a.m. 2 Rum relieves XI Cheshires & took over Trenches 118 – 120 Trenches. Very heavy bombardment by our Howitzers about 11.15 to 12. Noon.	
	13th		Enemy shells Ploegsteert in a full heph, and H.E. Shells exploded about 10 yards S.W. of Rifle House – a few windows broken Major A.H. Shead's village about 12-50 Came to field Sgt Cockayne was wounded by shell in Ploegsteert village — broken windows of bungalow. Pte 19 night, who went with him got through of 1.94 – Victim broken over & broken land — and Septemb. No less than 27 H.E. Shells dropped in and around Support Trench and Fire Trench 116.	

WAR DIARY
or
INTELLIGENCE SUMMARY

Army Form C. 2118

(Erase heading not required.)

Instructions regarding War Diaries and Intelligence Summaries are contained in F.S. Regs., Part II. and the Staff Manual respectively. Title Pages will be prepared in manuscript.

Place	Date	Hour	Summary of Events and Information	Remarks and references to Appendices
	14		Colonel E. W. Horne 3rd Bn. Seaforth Highlanders and Major J. W. Hess 20th Ballu. D.L.I. arrived for instructions. Major Hill was attached to C Coy in left Sub Section in Trenches.	
	15		ENEMY Shelly Supports and in vicinity of Rifles House (An Hevo 20) + damage done 2/8. 23 + 25" turned supply a switch by 103 Corps Heavy Artillery of 330 16" commenced damage turning cutting to assist in cutting but unfortunate Colonel E. W. Horne 3rd Bn. Seaforth Highlanders & Major J. W. Hess 20th L.J. left for return to ENGLAND at 17 a.m.	
	16			
	17		Relieved by L. Cheshires at 2. from NoB15549 Pte. J. O'Brien D.C.y. accidently wounded in billets - moving a flag to sept by L. Cheshire not of Room in which wounded - a round of ammunition taken attentively by L. Cheshire who clamp to have thrown it outside but unfortunate head burst & accidently wounding informant. Returnt R.A.M.C. Stopped on Duck Walk on way to medical Aid.	
	20		Lieut Thomas R.A.M.C. Stopped on Duck Walks removed to Hosps. About 9.30 a.m. Pvt Lady Scammons removed to Hosps. About 7 p.m. Message from Brigade Head Quarters saying that 9/C XI Cheshires who reported that Germans were turning goods on left sub section (Trenches 120) were given orders for all hands to man or equipment, have gas helmets ready, machine guns and out of these - men as well out of these - all turned out & wear accoutrements. and all wearing to Ha. Qn. at once where men's Ides - Estaminets were closed and men ordered to proceed to Battle Stations. About 8 p.m. order from 9/C Ha. Qn. that the alarm was a false - men to stand loose but keep of cacao to be kept during the night.	
	21		2/Lieut E. D. Daniel on arriving from England was taken in strength of Batt. posted to A Coy. Lieut J. S. Alexander R.A.M.C. reported his arrival to take over duty from Lieut Thomas R.A.M.C. admitted to Hosp. Vice Charge of the Batt.	

1875 Wt. W593/826 1,000,000 4/15 J.B.C. & A. A.D.S.S./Forms/C. 2118.

WAR DIARY or INTELLIGENCE SUMMARY

Army Form C. 2118

Place	Date	Hour	Summary of Events and Information	Remarks and references to Appendices
	21st Oct	10.45 am	No 14602 Pte J. Jennings "B" Coy wounded by bullet whilst filling sandbags. No 18703 Pte J. Howard "B" Coy wounded. Shot through thigh by bullet.	
		3.45 pm	About 3.45 pm Suffolks Coy over Hos Bn. front Quarters except two officers. Small party not from any company failed find any trench. Reported to Bde Qrs.	
	22nd		Lt Col A.G.B. King proceeded on leave to 29.10.15. Also Sgt Major J. Server – Leave commences 9.40 a.m.	
	23rd		Relieving Shropshire Regiment in Trenches 102-112 taking up the position during the night by 2nd South Lancashire Regt. The 2nd Bn. South Lancashire Regt taking up position previously occupied by us to G1, L1 2 Coy, Suffolks. Regt. taking 2 in scribes trenches 113 – 120. The Sk R. Latters hop on Bn. Regt. was 2nd Lancashire Regt on our left & Northampton during relief. Four officers & Troops Bis. Keynisby-Green was a water pipe 1943 & 3 Lucas Sapper C. Coy. So Keynisby 74 Butler as above. Sapper E Brook Sgt G & Co. A moved also Reynolds 11,963 Pte G. Butler D G return when opposite marked gun with rifle fire. Also wounded in arms by Mueller.	
	24th			
	25th		Christmas Day Hymns were sung. All recht other men with fraternise with phone over, ans to adopt tactics attitude this was strongly carried out. Very thing bombardment all day with minor disruption on high. This continues until 11 till two evening. But some gunpowder flew from our own camphor tons, and two enemy dire, laid low. During Bn. the hire was fired. The Orth was kept flying at left Must there have been Very loving, to the enemy. I am from Germans to Mars.	

WAR DIARY or INTELLIGENCE SUMMARY

Army Form C. 2118

Part IV

Place	Date	Hour	Summary of Events and Information	Remarks and references to Appendices
	26		in safety.	
	27		Trench 102. unwounded over to 74th Brigade at 9 a.m. & worked its way down Trench 103-112. About 7:30 a.m. the group deployed for the advance towards Fricourt station. The enemy trench system from our Regtl Hqrs from Shelter trench to Orchard Trench. Sept. ap. 149.63 Pages. Tk the a.B. wounded in shoulder & buttock. Relieved by Sgt Bates Br at 6:30 a.m. and returned to Regtl Hqrs Kiwi-Sgt Bates Quartier Cralin — a Cpl Toquet Rifle Grenadier in Peregrine now D Coy in trenches Farm. B/C Coy in trench in Peregrine Rout.	
			in Peregrine Peregrine Rout. 5th (...) during this time in Trench. Another man trying but with great (...) tried almost continuously. Reinfd going out at the each time. The men were very grateful even when they tried to him — (...) the men were very grateful. He almost single-handed flung with fire water pumps. Down (...) (...) return to trail out in the little warriors. He with smith a little more to train out (...) the trench. — He fell asleep alongside with me in the (...) enemy (...) ground among the (...) — (...) but it is any how nothing to do with it as it was returning to the line.	
	28		The afternoon was quiet being well into the Church Town Shutz Staffel Reports. There still exist trench Rifle Grenades & Signals were About 9:45 (...) Heavy Rifle machine gun fire rifle Grenades were opened on our Regtl Sect section. Down kept up for quite half an hour — about 4 of an hour from the reg'l office on French bombers and some return fire to abolish. All abt to be Church could hear had retired before till about Returned of the shells could be and were evidently from at enemy front line. So far so official what — (...) (...) (...) from in the enemy Meanwhile hello asleep — this Check Cairn	

WAR DIARY
or
INTELLIGENCE SUMMARY
(Erase heading not required.)

Army Form C. 2118

Instructions regarding War Diaries and Intelligence Summaries are contained in F. S. Regs, Part II. and the Staff Manual respectively. Title Pages will be prepared in manuscript.

Place	Date	Hour	Summary of Events and Information	Remarks and references to Appendices
	28 Cont.		to drop some where in Veerly & Sufferente. Three ended one by Bury Olical and dropped near Gp-Gps Here averted ares to break adrift from others were kent and dropped near the church. No damage reported.	
	29"		Lt Colonel A.G. Bh arq returned of leave.	
	30"		Nothing to report. Major Air Stewart left to proceed on leave from 31.12.15 to 7.1.16	
	31"		Nothing unusual.	

31st December 1915

R.G.M. Lang, Lieut Colonel
Commanding 87th ...

75th Inf. Bde.

25th Division

8th Battn.

SOUTH LANCASHIRE REGIMENT,

JANUARY, 1916.

Army Form C. 2118

WAR DIARY or INTELLIGENCE SUMMARY

8th Bn. South Lancashire Regiment

January 1916

Place	Date	Hour	Summary of Events and Information	Remarks and references to Appendices
Facteur Farm (Ploegsteert)	1st	6.30 am	Relieves 1st A.&S. Highlanders in Firing Line Trenches 113 to 120. Right Sub Section B Centre Sub Section C Coys, Left Sub Section D Company in Reserve – Hunters Avenue. Battalion on Right 9th Bn. South Lancashire Regt. Battalion on Left R. Innis. North Lancs.	
	2nd		Enemy shells trench N.W. of Estaminets on Convence. 75 Smoke H.E. Shells during the day. Otherwise very quiet. 2 O.R. of 60 arriving from some outposts of Coys. fallen in "Coy IN" out "IN" at 3 O.R. on C.Q. 3 N.C.Os + 28 men 8 Cos. INC 0+6 had three arrivals wdd 10 us from + went the Trench A20.	
	3rd		Enemy shells front trench – supports 117 – 120 and Hunters Avenue. The left Sub Section had one man hit in gun pit about 7.30am 5th Kings Coy. Capt J Harding returned to Line. 2/Lieut R.S. Pendlebury joined. Rapid fire bridge post 6 85.	
	4th		Brigade operations Artill. Trench Mortars. Rifle Grenades Machine Guns against Enemy Trenches Supports Communs 2.30 p Bombardment till about 3.30 PM (N. on left) about 3 pm enemy guns retaliated very heavy bombardment on our left front Trenches 119–120 occupied by C. Coy and supports 119 + 120 and back to Rifle House (Battalion Head Quarters) in all	

WAR DIARY or INTELLIGENCE SUMMARY

Place	Date	Hour	Summary of Events and Information	Remarks and references to Appendices
W.Cp.	4th Cont.		This Company fired between 400 & 500 shells over all calibres, from 3" guns to 6", while batteries firing S.E. pts. between J.120 & Support 120 fired 100 yards twenty or more times were cut short by shell fire — our C.O. gallantly turning C/V Coy owing to our Romm Heumen in firing trench - C/V Coy has two men S.D.P.H.E wounds 19/5603 Pte W. Mullen. one man strands to duty and one man Pte 19.815 Saunders H. from shock and Pte J.3745 Pte R. Kempt. C/E Seigel wound in Shrincits. 16426 Pte J.C. Webber K/E shell wound 15"851 Pte J.Y. Wied D.E. shell wound. The shelling was d Battalion Head Quarters was the heaviest we have yet had & escapes were marvelous as many a twelve shell haf [?] at the same time we went through the screen in Company Dug-out. Quite half a dozen tried to explode - in the Quite Room the Staff experienced quite a time — many being somewhere in dust & grit quite half a dozen times. The remainder of the night passed off very gl.J—	
	5th		During the forenoon the enemy was fairly actine with some salvo. The major J fyshil exchanged to the secondary Reserve - HUNTER AVENUE	

WAR DIARY or INTELLIGENCE SUMMARY

Army Form C. 2118

Place	Date	Hour	Summary of Events and Information	Remarks and references to Appendices
	6th		But no damage was done. Nothing exciting happened during remainder of the day time.	
	7th		Relieved by XI Cheshires.	
	8th		Nothing unusual occurred.	
	9th	10.18 9.20	Pte J Pedor OG wounded in thigh. Not at 6 am bullet lodged in thigh and removed in trip - Sent of Hope.	
		9.11.33	Pte C. Clee B. Coy wounded when with working party Capt of Hope to H of Hope	
			Maj A R Sturgel reported to trench. 10 officers & 95 others rank. New pass. relief of 9/10th Technicals. Relief 10.30	
		11.30	150 O.R. officers and men at 11.30 am, about 11.30 all but in	
		12.45 pm	Enemy Sgt Strafed our Pluegehunt Village all turned in	
			No damage reported. Our guns and mortars gave them 4 for 1.	
			Air - Three of our aeroplanes were brought down by Sept 12. 3	
			Hun aeroplanes. Three HE brought down in heavy AA fire 3	
			Quiet afternoon. After dark Huns reported Zell Naring	
			9 Sully reverses to Technical Schope Keithe.	
	10		Proceeded to Commune de Bois at Neuville	
			Enemy trench studies B & C Coys Hilton Pluegehunt work - one	
			HigW Explosive bursting in Rlg Officers Serg. Kitchen, 2 menkilled	
			Yet unfurled. Flemen killed were 14284 Pte Y Booby. 14386 Pte	
			Walesh R. G. wounded were 14931 Pte R Price 14446 Pte D Mihhell	
			14949 Pte of Davies 19059 Pte R Flores all Serious - Two	
			to the place about 9 pm there were two other Casualtie to 15th	
			Of the B.B.	

Place	Date	Hour	Summary of Events and Information	Remarks and references to Appendices
18th Ch°	Apt 5	3.0 p	The enemy opened with H.E. shell on Battery Pt. Ambs fire ceased 6.5pm - in all 15 shells were fired all of which were very close - two dropped in moat surrounding Sea Qrs (Sea fish were found on bridge) one 6 yards behind Orderly Room. The remainder quite close to Officers Mess. No damage done. No casualties. Several Offrs & B yer Sgt Mess with huts so named of pk. to guns. Col A/J B flag wire hit on bed with fragment of shell. Enemy aeroplane hover two times - Quietly. Enemy dropped a few shells in W.M. - no damage reported. Enemy flying of our S.S., very close, an aeroplane T attacked - Enemy front of him. S.S. very close, an aeroplane T by M chine gun but Sea was fairly active. Leonards by Machine gun fire were quite the only of the day -	Shrap T $H.E.$ $Eq. 936$
"		3.15pm	Major H.E. Branny Royal Horse Guards arrived at pt. of B Bay to take over command 1.Bn from Lt Col A.G B Laws, who is proceeding to ENGLAND. See Document to Centes on contemplation. — Major H.E. Branny assumes command from tomorrow 12/1/16	
12		7 am	Returns XI in Trenches. (Trenches 113-120.) Battalion Right	

WAR DIARY
or
INTELLIGENCE SUMMARY

(Erase heading not required.)

Army Form C. 2118

Place	Date	Hour	Summary of Events and Information	Remarks and references to Appendices
	13 Sept.		2nd Bn South Lancs Regt. Bn on left. Pl. Wilds afternoon Seaforth Highlanders.	
	14th		Pte. J. Denton. C.G. Killed. 14161 Pte C. Lanciers B.G	
			No. 15298 Pte J. Denton. " " "	
	15th		Killed.	
	16th		17162 Pte Cpl. J. DiSilvio C.G. wounded. to Hosp. 14979 Pte Brown B.G.Killed	
			Pte. Cpl. Wright " " "	
			No. 26254 Pte Jn. Robinson B.G. " " "	
			" 13970 " J. Lloyd B.G. " " "	
			" 15983 " W. Cairns B.G. " " "	
			" 13977 L.Cpl. R. Earles C.G. " " "	
	18th		" 15414 Pte S. Earles C.G. Killed	
	17th		Return by XI Am. and returned to Reserve Billets at Freelen	
	18th		No. 15414 Pte S. Earles C.G. Killed.	
	22		Enemy heavily shelled the vicinity of Bn. H.A. Gas H.E. & Shrapnel commenced about 9.30 ceases 9.35 - resumed about 10.10 and ceases about 10.35 - altogether about 50 shells were fired	
	23rd		No Casualties returning	
			Received by XI Chisham in Trench	
	27th		No. 14551 Qu.G. Burrows B.G. wounded	
			Relieved by XI Royal Scots 7 am. am. Bn. returned to Reserve Billets at Steenwerk	

WAR DIARY
or
INTELLIGENCE SUMMARY

Army Form C. 2118

Place	Date	Hour	Summary of Events and Information	Remarks and references to Appendices
	28th		Armoured Trains Company of one Officer and 9 other ranks sent to take over Buicks at Steenwerck. Advance Party - Horse lasts arrived to take over Buicks for Cavalry.	
	29		Bn. moved off at 6.30 am for Steenwerck. arrived about 1.30 pm. at Bleuka.	
Couterroix	30		Moved off at 6 am for Couterroix and arrived about 1 pm. Bn. in Buicks.	
	31		Nothing unusual.	

H. Brany
J.R. Crispel
Lt Col
Commanding 8 Souslaves Rgt

75th Inf. Bde.

25th Division

8th Battn.

SOUTH LANCASHIRE REGIMENT

FEBRUARY, 1916.

8th S. Lancs
26   Vol: 5

75

Army Form C. 2118

WAR DIARY
or
INTELLIGENCE SUMMARY
(Erase heading not required.)

Instructions regarding War Diaries and Intelligence Summaries are contained in F.S. Regs., Part II. and the Staff Manual respectively. Title Pages will be prepared in manuscript.

Place	Date	Hour	Summary of Events and Information	Remarks and references to Appendices
Couekcuik	May 1919		On Corps Rest Fields. Company Training. Lighting. Rapid Loading, Bombing, Bayonet Fighting. Route marches to divine service. Company entrenchments.	
	2		— do — — do —	
	3		— do — — do —	
	4		— do — — do —	
	5		— do — Concert at Battalion	
			Hd. Qrs. — a Great Success. Divine Service.	
	6		Nothing unusual.	
	7		Inspection by Corps Commander. Very satisfactory	
	8		Lord Kitchener expresses Lunch by Thanks	
	9		Divisional Semi Final match York v. — III Cheshires — last at 6. South Lancashire B & Scots to meet.	
	10		Lut. W. t. Hutton arrived from France having posted to Bn. from 10th Bn. in England.	
	11		Went by G.S. Scriven proceeded to 10 am. Home Establishment	
	21			

1875 Wt. W593/826 1,000,000 4/15 J.B.C. & A. A.D.S.S./Forms/C. 2118.

WAR DIARY
or
INTELLIGENCE SUMMARY

Army Form C. 2118

(Erase heading not required.)

Place	Date	Hour	Summary of Events and Information	Remarks and references to Appendices
	28		Chief Major Watson appointed Acting Regt/Sergt Major Rice Service. Battalion Daily exercise in Route marching, Bayonet fighting, Wire work &c &c.	
	29		Bugle Cross Country Race Battalion took 2nd & 3rd Prize. at Boxing Contest Sergt Duckhouse won Heavy weight. Tug of war Sergt Tort 3rd Feversier beat team at Mr A. W. Sheuts appointment as 2nd in Command expiring from 27 Oct 1915.	

H Sweeney
Lieut Colonel
Commanding 8 Southern R?

75th Inf. Bde.

25th Division

8th Battn.

SOUTH LANCASHIRE REGIMENT,

MARCH, 1916.

25

8 S. Lancs
vol. 6

Army Form C. 2118

WAR DIARY
or
INTELLIGENCE SUMMARY

(Erase heading not required.)

Shruyh 1 March 30 G.R. 98/3

Instructions regarding War Diaries and Intelligence Summaries are contained in F. S. Regs., Part II. and the Staff Manual respectively. Title Pages will be prepared in manuscript.

Place	Date	Hour	Summary of Events and Information	Remarks and references to Appendices
Courte	1		Nothing unusual.	
Crest	2			
Diever	4		Q.Master Lylm Lieut W.H. Train proceeded to England in charge of Strength of Bn. accompts.	
Rest Billets	5 & 6		Usual Training.	
	7		Capt. Devlin (Adjutant) struck transferred to Guard List and Lieutenant G. Struik off Battalion. 2.Lt. W. Luscombe (1st Royal Dragoons) joined as Adjutant.	
	8 & 9		Nothing unusual.	
Thiennes	10		Brigade moved Southwards to join the 17th Corps in 3rd Army. Moved by Road to THIENNES.	
Ammettes	11		Brigade marched on to Ammettes. AMMETTES.	
	12,13,14		Brigade remained halted. 2Lt J.N. DARLINGTON and 2Lt A. McCULLOCH joined the Battalion (13th).	
Hesdrus	15		Brigade marched to HESTRUS.	
	16		Battalion remained halted. 2 Lt J.E. HIBBERT rejoined the Battalion from Sick leave.	
Marquay	17		Battalion marched to MARQUAY in 5th Corps area.	
	18-22		Nothing unusual.	

Army Form C. 2118

WAR DIARY
or
INTELLIGENCE SUMMARY
(Erase heading not required.)

March 1916

Instructions regarding War Diaries and Intelligence Summaries are contained in F. S. Regs., Part II. and the Staff Manual respectively. Title Pages will be prepared in manuscript.

II

Place	Date	Hour	Summary of Events and Information	Remarks and references to Appendices
Marquay	23		2 i/c, Adjutant & 1 Coy Commander with IX Bde Staff visited Subsidiary line of Southern Corps front.	Seat of Pte [?]
Marquay	24+25		Nothing unusual. The British remained in Corps Reserve.	
	26		2 i/c, Adjutant & 1 Coy Commander went to the Staff visited the northern sector of the Embusbury line, taken over by the XVII Corps.	
do	27+30		Nothing unusual. The Batt. remained in Corps Reserve.	
do	31		The Battalion was inspected by the Brigadier in Chief, the 154th was strong. Close mass drill, the C in C expressed his approval. & also this opinion that close order drill was the one thing that is now the day.	

H. Mainey Lt. Col
Cmg 8 "South Lancashire Regt"

75th Inf. Bde.

25th Division

8th Battn.

SOUTH LANCASHIRE REGIMENT,

APRIL, 1916.

WAR DIARY or INTELLIGENCE SUMMARY

Army Form C. 2118

8 S. Lancs

XXV

Strength 1st April 1916

Place	Date	Hour	Summary of Events and Information	Remarks and references to Appendices
Bruay	1		Nothing unusual. Battn remaining in Corps Reserve.	
do	2		2/Lieut W.D. CORNISH invalided to England on account of strength of the strength.	
do	3,4,5		Draft: 1 Sergeant & 83 other ranks, taken on the strength, the 2nd reinf from ETAPLES	
do	5		Nothing unusual. Battn remaining in Corps Reserve.	
do	6		2/Lieut R.M. TREVETHAN & 15 other ranks from ETAPLES & taken on the strength this date. Lieut Revd J. Lycell from the 1st Battn + taken on the strength this date.	
do	7,12,13		Nothing unusual. Battn remaining in Corps Reserve.	
do	14		The Brigade was inspected by the G.O.C. 11th Corps, who expressed his pleasure at the turn out of the Battn, particularly at the condition of the transport.	
do	15		Capt E.C. Jarvis joined the Battn from ETAPLES & taken on the strength this date.	
do	16,17,20		Nothing unusual. Battn remaining in Corps Reserve.	
ECOIVRES	21		The Battn marched to ECOIVRES & went into Divisional Reserve.	
do	22,27		Remained in Divisional Reserve, the Battn furnishing Rigging Parties up the front line communication trenches, & Lts WATSON, WOODHOUSE & DAVIDSON joined the Battn. MAJOR STUART admitted to Hospital Sick.	
0.61.60.62	28		The Battn took over the line 0.60 to 0.62 due EAST of NEUVILLE ST VAAST	
do	29		The enemy was very active with Trench MORTARS + BOMBS at 1.5 P.M. the enemy blew up a mine bringing 3 men of C Company + wounding 3 other ranks	

WAR DIARY or INTELLIGENCE SUMMARY

Army Form C. 2118

(Erase heading not required.)

Place	Date	Hour	Summary of Events and Information	Remarks and references to Appendices
O.60 & O.62	29		2 Lieut S.G.T EARLE was admitted to Hospital from shock. Wounded 19993 Pte N.TRAVIS. 12563 Pte A.MELLOR & 13316 Pte A.STUBBS. admitted 19393 C.S.M. J. GOULDING. 15512 Sergt D.DUCKHOUSE & 15573 Pte H.V. ROSE, owing to the rush of events it was impossible to ascertain the names of the remaining who were undoubtedly killed by the explosion.	
Do	30		The enemy artillery was very active, shelling D Coy support posts in CRUMP. One man was wounded 14513 Pte E.STRONG. The remainder of the day unoppressed in the exchange of Trench Mortars etc.	

H Beasley - Lt Col
Comd'g 6" Batt'n South Lanc Regt

75th Inf. Bde.

25th Division

8th Battn.

SOUTH LANCASHIRE REGIMENT,

MAY, 1916.

WAR DIARY or INTELLIGENCE SUMMARY

Army Form C. 2118

MAY 1916 1/S Lancs Regt

Strength on 1st May — Officers 41, Other ranks 984

Place	Date	Hour	Summary of Events and Information	Remarks and references to Appendices
NEUVILLE ST VAAST O.60.50.62 Trenches	1		The enemy again active with Trench MORTARS & Heavy guns doing a lot of damage to Communication Trenches.	8
"	2		Very heavy shelling trenches badly damaged Casualties 3 wounded 14956 Pte W.King, 14609 Pte Waterbury & 14939 Pte Roberts.	
"	3		Enemy very active with Trench Mortars & Aerial Torpedoes great amount of damage to trenches Casualties 4 wounded on of which died of wounds 14593 Cpl C Woods, 17092 McJLarkin, 6105 Pte J.Wray died of wounds.	
"	4		Enemy commenced at daybreak assist H.E. Shells Trench Mortars & Aerial Torpedoes. Rifle Grenades Casualties LIEUT A.N.MORRIS, wounded & 4 other ranks 15299 Sergt Moore 15289 Pte Barlow, 13196 Pte Menyys 14631 Pte Davies.	
NEUVILLE ST VAAST	5 & 10		Battn relieved by the 2 Battn South Lancs and moved to NEUVILLE ST VAAST in Brigade reserve from 5th to 10th Casualties 10679 Sergt THOMAS 11990 Pte Winterbottom Draft of 30 N.C.O & men received from ETAPLES.	
Trenches	11		Relieved 2 Battn South Lancs in Trenches O.61 to O.62 Casualties 10801 Pte Bleese wounded. Enemy very active with Artillery.	
"	12		Enemy very active with Trench Mortars & H.E Casualties 10466 Pte Golding died of wounds & 19397 Pte Phipps wounded. The whole of the Coys not on Sentry employed in digging new line of defence & repairing the Trenches after Heavy shell fire.	8A

Army Form C. 2118

WAR DIARY
or
INTELLIGENCE SUMMARY
(Erase heading not required.)

Instructions regarding War Diaries and Intelligence Summaries are contained in F.S. Regs., Part II. and the Staff Manual respectively. Title Pages will be prepared in manuscript.

Place	Date	Hour	Summary of Events and Information	Remarks and references to Appendices
Trenches	13		Enemy ordnance very active, with Shrapnel, H.E. our artillery did great damage to their trenches, wounded 2Lt Pte J. Knell.	
"	14 / 15 / 16		Enemy very active with Trench Mortars, aerial Torpedoes & rifle grenades, Battn busily employed in repairing trenches & digging new communication trenches, guns received that LIEUT MORRIS died of wounds on the 12 inst. Battn relieved on the night of the 15th by the 2 Batn South Lancs. at 2 p.m. then remained in PARALLEL VIII until 9pm & then proceeded trench digging, afterwards marching back to ECOIVRES in divisional Reserve.	
ECOIVRES	17 / 18 / 19 / 20		On Divisional Reserve at ECOIVRES. The Battn finding digging parties at AIX NIETZ & to FOUCHE. Casualties, 2 Jn 17531 Pte Harris 1764, 7 Pte R. Roberts wounded.	
Trenches	20		The Battn took over the Trenches about 10 pm, enemy rather quiet, a little exchange of grenades.	
"	21		Nothing unusual occured, 25 Pyganies continuing wiring up Rosenrhat Line & building up the Resistance Line.	

Army Form C. 2118

WAR DIARY
or
INTELLIGENCE SUMMARY

(Erase heading not required.)

Instructions regarding War Diaries and Intelligence Summaries are contained in F. S. Regs., Part II. and the Staff Manual respectively. Title Pages will be prepared in manuscript.

Place	Date	Hour	Summary of Events and Information	Remarks and references to Appendices
Trenches	22		Enemy shelling very heavily, a great amount of damage was done to the trenches. Our Trench Mortars & Rifle Grenades did good. Also message to the Enemies Mines & on hostile Artilleries retaliated & silenced their guns. Casualties 2 wounded 1147 Pte Dean, 1859 Pte Donnelley, 3192 Lce Cpl McWilliam & 1999 Pte Dickinson.	
"	23		Enemy again very active with T.M. & Rifle Grenades which were silenced by our Grenadiers. 1 killed & 3 wounded 14960 Sergt Bridge Killed 1469 & 1 Sergt M°Kently 18894 Pte French & 19121 Pte Spendsman Wounded.	
"	24		Nothing unusual occurred, quiet. An exchange of T.M. & Rifle Grenades Casualties 14162 L/Cpl Higgins wounded. The Batt" was relieved by the 2nd Batt" about 10 p.m. & returned to their cellars in NEUVILLE St. VAAST. Brigade Reserve.	
NEUVILLE ST VAAST	25 to 30		The Batt" in 18th Reserve supplying two companies working under the direction of the R.E. officers & the other two doing carrying parties & various fatigues. Casualties 15488 Pte Boyd, Killed 15435 Pte Hallsworth died of wounds 15453 Pte Rocholl wounded 14088 Pte Boyley Killed. The undermentioned Officers joined the Batt" on the 29th inst. 2 Lieuts J. W. Byrne, H.H. Reely, Sudgrove. J. Cumming. J.R.T.P. Morgan, W.J. Thorn, H.P. Pleasock & A. Ferguson.	
"			J R Buckney, H C L T/ Col Com 5 South Lanc	

75th Inf. Bde.

25th Division

8th Battn.

SOUTH LANCASHIRE REGIMENT,

JUNE, 1916.

WAR DIARY or INTELLIGENCE SUMMARY

Army Form C. 2118

June 1916

Place	Date	Hour	Summary of Events and Information	Remarks and references to Appendices
BERNEUIL	19" to 24"		At BERNEUIL arriving on the morning of the 19"inst". The Batt" continued Training. 2/Lieut H. WATTS joined the Batt", as Transport Officer.	
TALMAS	25" 26" 27"		Brigade continuing the march South, arriving at TALMAS on the 25" & stayed 3 days.	
TOUTENCOURT	28 29 30		Continued moving South arriving at TOUTENCOURT. The Batt" billetted in huts & remained there until the night of the 30" when the Batt" again moved, marching by night, arriving at HEDAUVILLE in the morning of the 1" July 1916.	

H Bruey Lt Col.
Comdg 2" South Wales

75/   8 S Lancs June
25   June 1916   Army Form C. 2118   Officers other Ranks 2118
                  WAR DIARY   Stringth   41   985
                       or
                  INTELLIGENCE SUMMARY
                  (Erase heading not required.)   9A

Instructions regarding War Diaries and Intelligence
Summaries are contained in F. S. Regs., Part II.
and the Staff Manual respectively. Title Pages
will be prepared in manuscript.

Place	Date	Hour	Summary of Events and Information	Remarks and references to Appendices
NEVILLE ST VAAST	1		Battn in Brigade Reserve, supplying digging & carrying parties, Normally on 13th/14th Sergt PREWIN wounded.	
ACQ	2		Battn was relieved by the 7/8 Argyle & Sutherland Highlanders & marched to billets in ACQ.	
BETHONSART	3 to 14		Battn marched from ACQ & proceeded to billeting area for training, on the night of the 14/15th the Brigade was joined to the G.H.Q. reserve restrained Brigade & Divisional	
AVERDOINGT			Brigade marched on the 14th/15th from the X Corps & "Army, arriving at AVERDOINGT. Billeted for 1 night 14/15 inst. The Brigade resumed the march & the Battn billetted at FORTEL the night of the 15th/16/14.	
FORTEL			The Battn marched by night arriving at BEAUMETZ on the morning of the 18th inst- 2° Lt. B.M.GREEN & J.S.JONES joined the Battn.	
BEAUMETZ			The Battn again marched at night from BEAUMETZ to	

1875. Wt. W593/826 1,000,000 4/15 J.B.C. & A. A.D.S.S./Forms/C. 2118.

75th Bde.
25th Divi.

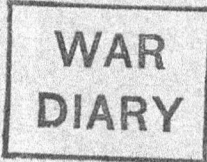

8th BATTALION

SOUTH LANCASHIRE REGIMENT.

JULY 1916

8th Bn. South Lancs Regt   8.S. Lancs July

Army Form C. 2118

WAR DIARY
or
INTELLIGENCE SUMMARY
(Erase heading not required.)

Vol 10

Place	Date	Hour	Summary of Events and Information	Remarks and references to Appendices
HEDAUVILLE	2		Left HEDAUVILLE for AVELUY WOOD where at 11.30 p.m. for the trenches SOUTH of THIEPVAL as support to the other Battalions of the Brigade in the attack in the German line carried out at 6.15 a.m. July 3rd. The Bn	
	3		took over the line from Johnsons Post to HAMILTON AVENUE and on the night of the 3/4 July the Bn took over the line held by	
	4		the 2nd Bn. So. Lancs Regt. The Duke of Wellingtons Worcesters Regt. T.F. being on our left and the 8th Border Regt on our right.	(3)
	5		On the night of the 4/5 July the Bn was relieved by the 7th Worcester Regt and went back to AVELUY WOOD. The Bn bivouacked	
	6		here for two days	
	7		The Bn moved to UNSA TARA trenches by day via BRU&FIX Corner NORTH of ALBERT arriving there about 5.30 p.m. The Bn stayed there until 11.30 p.m. and then moved to take up	
	8A		position for an attack on Germans line just SOUTH of OVILLERS to the RIDGE SOUTH of NASH VALLEY and NORTH of LA BOISSELLE. The Bn attacked about 4 A.M. and took the front line	10A

WAR DIARY or INTELLIGENCE SUMMARY

Army Form C. 2118

Place	Date	Hour	Summary of Events and Information	Remarks and references to Appendices
OVILLERS	8		Trench practically without opposition. Touch was obtained with the EAST SUSSEX on our left and the 11th Lancasters Fusiliers on our right. During the day we occupied the German front line trench as far as a point about 150 yards SOUTH of the SOUTHERN edge of OVILLERS and a part of the 2nd line trench as far as Point 18. (Ref 1/5000 TRENCH MAP)	
	9		During the day the work of consolidating the ground gained was continued and about 5.30 p.m. a covering attack on point 24 (Ref 1/5000 TRENCH MAP) was made & supported by two platoons attacking from different directions but was unsuccessful. At 8 p.m. in pursuance of direct orders from Bde. an attempt was made to capture the remainder of German 2nd line trench determined rush across the open. This attack did not reach its objective owing to heavy machine gun fire from VILLERS which completely enfiladed the ground to be crossed and the enormous condition of the ground due to recent heavy rainfall.	

WAR DIARY
or
INTELLIGENCE SUMMARY

Army Form C. 2118

Place	Date	Hour	Summary of Events and Information	Remarks and references to Appendices
VILLERS	9		On the night of the 9/10 July the Bn Bombers co-operated in an attack by one company of the 11th Cheshires on point 74. This attack was not pushed owing to strong opposition being encountered. The Bn were then relieved by the 11th Cheshires and went back to the UNSA TARA LINE where they stayed until the night of the 12/13 July.	
	10			
	12			
	13		About 12.30 a.m. the Bn moved up to the line in support of the 8th Borders and 2nd Bn So Lancs. At 4 a.m. two Companies B and D were called upon to make an attack to try and push through OVILLERS. The NORTHERN end of the village was reached but as the right flank was in the air and the Bn was being enfiladed by machine guns they retired to the centre of the village and there dug themselves in. At this time a Bn of the Worcesters (T.F.) were on our left and	

1875 Wt. W593/826 1,000,000 4/15 J.B.C.&A. A.D.S.S./Forms/C. 2118.

WAR DIARY
or
INTELLIGENCE SUMMARY
(Erase heading not required.)

Army Form C. 2118

Place	Date	Hour	Summary of Events and Information	Remarks and references to Appendices
OVILLERS	13		The 7TH Bde on our right (8 A.M.). The rest of the day was spent in consolidating this line	
	14		On the night of 14/15 the Br School by ready to our Frontages were to the troops on our right (there no and obtained touch with us. This they failed to do and the Bn did not move from its position	
	15			
	16		In pursuance of orders from Bde H.Qrs, a bombing attack was organised to take point 63 (REF 1/5000 TRENCH MAP in which Stokes Mortar and Rifle Grenades were used in support. Point 63 was captured about 2.30 pm. The attack commencing at 12.45 p.m. The position was consolidated and all the enemy could be seen moving to the right and firing themselves up. About 2.30 a.m. the Commanding Officer Lt. Col. H. Brassey (Major Royal Horseguards) was killed by a rifle bullet. Lieut. J. Adam the Bn was relieved by the Worcesters (7.P.)	
SENLIS	17		and moved to SENLIS where it bivouaced for the day awaiting	

WAR DIARY
or
INTELLIGENCE SUMMARY

(Erase heading not required.)

Army Form C. 2118.

Instructions regarding War Diaries and Intelligence Summaries are contained in F.S. Regs., Part II and the Staff Manual respectively. Title Pages will be prepared in manuscript.

Place	Date	Hour	Summary of Events and Information	Remarks and references to Appendices
SENLIS	17/6		5 pm moved to HEDAUVILLE where it bivouacked for the night.	
AMPLIER	18/6		The Bn moved by day to AMPLIER into hutments where it remained until three days	
LOUVENCOURT	20/6 22/6		The Bn moved by day to LOUVENCOURT where it remained until next day	
ACHEUX	23/6		The Bn moved by day to ACHEUX WOOD into hutments where it remained two days	
AUCHONVILLERS TRENCHES	25/6 29/6		The Bn moved into support trenches occupying TRENCHES 86 and 88 and garrisoning AUCHONVILLERS. About 1.30 p.m. 29 July the Bn relieved 2nd Bn So Staffs in the front line taking over the line from BROADWAY on the	
	6		right to JACOBS LADDER on the left.	
	31			

23/6/16

A M Henderson Lt Col
Commdg 8 Sherwood R

MESSAGES AND SIGNALS.

Prefix	Code	m.	Words	Charge	This message is on a/c of:	Recd. at	m
Office of Origin and Service Instructions.			Sent		...........Service.	Date	
			At......m.			From	
			To		(Signature of "Franking Officer.")	By	
			By				

TO { M.P.

Sender's Number.	Day of Month.	In reply to Number.	
* 1638	4	BM 675	AAA

(1) The battalion was in support to the brigade and did not take part in the attack.

(a) Our losses were entirely from shell fire, the trenches being very much broken down.

(b) The opposing troops were driven back mainly by shell fire and machine gun fire on the supporting lines as they crossed the open.

(c) I cannot answer. The enemy kept a very enfilade fire from the right of the attack.

From	H Brassey Lt. Col.
Place	Commdg 8th Bn S Lancs Regt.
Time	

The above may be forwarded as now corrected. (Z)

....
Censor. Signature of Addressor or person authorised to telegraph in his name.

* This line should be erased if not required.

325,000. W 14042—M 44. H. W. & V., Ld. 12/15.

75th Brigade.
25th Diviwion

1/8th BATTALION

SOUTH LANCASHIRE REGIMENT

AUGUST 1 9 1 6

25. Army. Form C. 2118.
August
8 S. Lancs
VOL 11

WAR DIARY
or
INTELLIGENCE SUMMARY

8 Gth So Lancs Regt

Place	Date	Hour	Summary of Events and Information	Remarks and references to Appendices
BEAUMONT HAMEL	July 30		Relieved 2nd So Lancs Regt in firing and support lines opposite BEAUMONT HAMEL	
	Aug 5		Relieved by 2nd So Lancs Regt. Withdrew into Divisional Reserve in MAILLY MAILLY WOOD	
	8		Moved into billets at BEAUSART	
	9		Handed billets over to 3rd Grenadier Guards and marched about 7 p.m. to WARNIMONT WOOD	
	15		Trained in WARNIMONT WOOD. Working parties (2 boys) at FORCEVILLE and VARENNES	
	15		MARCHED to RAINCHEVAL	
	17		Marched to FORCEVILLE	
	18		Marched to Bois DAVELUY - 320 digging opposite THIEPVAL night - Assaulting trenches	
	21		MARCHED back to FORCEVILLE	
	22 to 25		Trained there	

WAR DIARY
or
INTELLIGENCE SUMMARY

Army Form C. 2118.

Place	Date	Hour	Summary of Events and Information	Remarks and references to Appendices
FORCEVILLE	25		Sports and a camp fire concert	
AUTHUILLE	26		Into firing and support line in front of AUTHUILLE relieving 10th Cheshire Regt.	
LEIPSIC SALIENT	27		Into firing and support line of LEIPSIC SALIENT relieving 8th L.N. LANCS Regt	
	28		At 4 P.M. attacked the enemy salient. D Company on right on front 69 to point 68 advanced N.W. in two waves on front 48. D Coy was stopped by shrapnel barrage all its officers wounded and its commander Captain Jarvis killed. B Coy got into German trench fired one dug out but was forced out. B Company Commander Captain Grimsdell was seriously wounded. Attack failed.	
	29		H Q dug out of C Coy hit by a shell 5 killed and 8 wounded	
	30		Heavy rain	
	31		An officers patrol (~~Recce~~ Foot ~~D/R~~) Guards captured by L Company	

13 Sept. 16

M. Richardson Lt Col
Comdg 8th June R

75th. INFANTRY BDE.

25th. DIVISION

8th. SOUTH LANCS REGT.

S E P T E M B E R 1 9 1 6.

WAR DIARY
INTELLIGENCE SUMMARY

Army Form C. 2118.

(Erase heading not required.)

Place	Date 1916	Hour	Summary of Events and Information	Remarks and references to Appendices
LEIPSIC REDOUBT	Sept 1st		Clearing trenches. At night caught an enemy patrol by a ruse — using his Very light signal. Heavily shelled.	
	2nd			
	3rd	5.10AM	Ordered to support 1st Wilts. R. in its attack on Turk Trench did so. A. Coy went to assistance of 3rd Worc. R. attacking pt 45.	
		Evening	Relieved by Border R. went back to Black Horse B. into dug-outs	
	4th		Moved into dug-outs at CRUCIFIX Corner	
	5th		Marched back to BOUZINCOURT — tents	
	7th		" " ACHEUX — huts	
	8th		Draft (80) from Cheshire R. joined. Poorly trained.	
	9th		Marched to AMPLIER — huts	
	10th		" " BERNAVILLE — billets	
	11th		" " CRAMONT — "	
	12th		Began training at CRAMONT and started to refit	
	13th		Draft (85) Shropshire L.I. (Territorials) joined. Good.	
	17		Marched to AMPLIER — 39 fell out — new boots & new drawers.	
	25th		" " ACHEUX — Draft of 100 from S. Lanc. R. joined, mixed Territorials and Regulars. Training a New pun. also arrived.	
	26th		Marched to BOUZINCOURT — bivouacked	
	29th		Dumped packs. Marched to DULLERS. Spent plug there. At 7 P.M. left KAY Dump (POZIERES) and went into ZOLLERN Redoubt and HESSIAN Tr relieving right unit of 32nd Inf Bridge	
	30th	7P.M.	M.M.P's heardson 8.5 Linc. R.	

75th Inf. Bde.

25th Division.

8th Battn.

SOUTH LANCASHIRE REGIMENT,

OCTOBER, 1916.

Army Form C. 2118.

WAR DIARY
or
INTELLIGENCE SUMMARY

(Erase heading not required.)

618th South Lancs Regt

Place	Date	Hour	Summary of Events and Information	Remarks and references to Appendices
ZOLLERN Redoubt & HESSIAN Trench	Oct.'16 1st		D.Company sent bombing squad and assisted Canadians when they failed to hold REGINA Trench. Also gave them bombs & S.A.A.	
	3rd	6A.M.	Relieved in ZOLLERN Redoubt at MOUQUET Fm. Draft of Cheshire Yeomanry joined	
	4th		Into PICCADILLY trench relieving P.P.C.L.I.	
	6th		Battalion moved back to BOUZINCOURT	
	9th		Working party (375) to CRUCIFIX corner	
	10/11		Night – Working party under Captain Reade dug between SCHWABEN & STUFF Redoubts, a new front line (DANUBE & trenches)	
	15th		Battalion moved into support lines behind STUFF Redoubt –	
	18th		took over HESSIAN trench with object of taking REGINA. Heavy rain; Attack on REGINA postponed	
	19th		Carried dumps forward "	
	20th		" – 2 Companies went back to DANUBE Tr.	
	21st	7.30 A.M.	Companies from DANUBE went into HESSIAN	
		12.6	The Battalion in 4 waves – first 2 extended last 2 in lines of half platoons in file – advanced from HESSIAN with the 8th Border R. on	

WAR DIARY
or
INTELLIGENCE SUMMARY

(Erase heading not required.)

Army Form C. 2118.

8/13th South Lancs Regt/-

Place	Date	Hour	Summary of Events and Information	Remarks and references to Appendices
HEM.	22nd 23rd 24th 26th		its right & the 2nd S. Lanc. I.R. on its left, Battalion bombers on the left moved down STUMP Road. The German infantry was found in its dug-outs in REGINA Trench and in STUMP Road. The bombers who went down STUMP as per as our artillery would allow shot from 50 to 100 issuing from dug-outs. About 150 to 200 surrendered to the rest of the Battalion. Our casualties were 1 Officer killed, 1 missing & 6 wounded and in other ranks 25 killed 42 missing 85 wounded. Relieved by 10th Worc. R. went into bivouacs near BOUZINCOURT moved to WARLOY - 300 in busses, remainder a-foot. " " HEM - 150 in busses, remainder a-foot. Major W.J. Hashett-Smith, Royal Irish Rifles, attached 2nd South Lancs Regt- assumed temporary command of the Battalion in the absence of Lt Col A.J. Richardson D.S.O.	
	25th		Inspection by the Army Commander, General Sir H. de la P. Gough, K.C.B who congratulated the Battalion on their work in the recent operations. (Oct 1916)	

Army Form C. 2118.

WAR DIARY
or
INTELLIGENCE SUMMARY
(Erase heading not required.)

Place	Date	Hour	Summary of Events and Information	Remarks and references to Appendices
	30th	3.19 A.M.	The Battalion entrained at DOULLENS SOUTH STN for BAILLEUL.	
		2.30	Arrived in Billets in the neighbourhood of SCHAEKKEN —	
	31st		SCHAEKKEN —	

w/ Herbert Smith Major
O/c 8th 13th South Lancs Regt
31.10.16.

75th Inf. Bde.

25th Division

8th Battn.

SOUTH LANCASHIRE REGIMENT,

NOVEMBER, 1916.

Army Form C. 2118.

WAR DIARY
or
INTELLIGENCE SUMMARY
(Erase heading not required.)

8 S Lanc R¹
Vol 14

Place	Date	Hour	Summary of Events and Information	Remarks and references to Appendices
SCHAEXKEN	1916 Nov 1.11.16	3.30 A.M.	Battalion marched to PONT-de-NIEPPE. In billets at OOST-JOVE FARM. Crossed FRANCO-BELGIAN border BELGIUM.	
BAILLEUL	2.11.16		Battalion relieved 2.8th (Leicesters) R.W. Surrey Regt in support less to 2/13th S. Lanc Regt & 11th Cheshires on Hill 63 - PLOEGSTEERT Wood. A. Coy Right Sector U.14.B.4.6. 15. T18.6.05.25 - 12. Coy Left Sector T18.a.8.5. 10. Tr.a.7.4 - C.Cy. RED LODGE + D. Coy at DONEGAL ST. B.H.Q. at RED LODGE - PLOEGSTEERT WOOD.	
	6th	2 P.M.	Battalion relieved 2nd Bn S. Lanc R. in Front Line DOUVE Sector, C & D Coys in Front Line A & B Coys in Support relieved C & D	
	11th	" "	Relieved by 2nd Bn S.L.R. in Front Line, C Coy took over Forts on Hill 63. Remainder into Reg-out at HYDE PARK Corner. Issued with small Box Respirators.	
	14th	" "		
	16th	10AM	Relieved 2nd Bn " " in Front Line. A & B Coys in Front Line	
	20th	2PM	C & D Coys relieved A & B.	
	23rd			
	26th to 30th	10AM	Relieved by 2nd Bn went into Reg-out HYDE PARK CORNER. A Coy to Forts. Training i. from Tennis, Rifle Practice, Bomb throwing, Handling Arms, also worked on Firing Line and carried.	

2nd Dec 1916

M J Winterbottom Lt Col
Commdg 8th S. Lanc. R.

14A

75th Inf. Bde.

25th Division

8th Battn.

SOUTH LANCASHIRE REGIMENT,

DECEMBER, 1916.

Army Form C. 2118.

8 S Lancer Rgt

WAR DIARY
or
INTELLIGENCE SUMMARY
(Erase heading not required.)

Instructions regarding War Diaries and Intelligence Summaries are contained in F.S. Regs., Part II. and the Staff Manual respectively. Title Pages will be prepared in manuscript.

Vol 15

Place	Date	Hour	Summary of Events and Information	Remarks and references to Appendices
PLOEGSTEERT.	2/1/16			
"	5/12/16		Relieved 2nd Batt in front line – C & B Coys firing line –	
"	6/12/16		Relieved by 13th R Inn.is Fus: went into dug outs at HYDE PARK CORNER – B Coy into huts	
"	7,8,9		Relieved by 9th R Innis Fus: went to ROMARIN – into huts there –	
			Drill & training –	
	10th		Relieved 2nd Batt in right sub sector (1 Bde – South of PLOEGSTEERT – A & B Coys in firing line – H.Q at DE MISON 14.75.	
	13th		C & D Coys relieved A & B Coys.	
	15th		TM & fumes (in their fields) wire cutting –	
	16th		Relieved by 2nd Batt – went into supports at PLOEGSTEERT HALL, TOUQUET BERTHE and huts in HUNTERS AVENUE (B Coy in huts).	
	22nd		Relieved 2nd Batt in front line – C & D Coys in firing line – Lt Col Richardson DSO handed the command to Lt Col Smith	
	23rd		C & D Coy relieved A & B Coys respectively –	
	28th		Lt & B on att 2? to 2? Third – A no night of front Relieved by 2nd S. Lancs in front line, we then went to ROMARIN CAMP.	
	29th 30th		Lt Col Smith handed over command to Major Robinson D.S.O.	
	31st		Training –	

15A

WAR DIARY
INTELLIGENCE SUMMARY

Place	Date	Hour	Summary of Events and Information	Remarks and references to Appendices
Romarin	2.1.17		2nd S.Lanc relieved us at ROMARIN CAMP. We moved into DE SEULE Camp, and CARTER CAMP.	

W.J Robinson (?)
Comd.
8 Loyal Regt

Army Form C. 2118.

WAR DIARY
or
INTELLIGENCE SUMMARY

(Erase heading not required.)

Instructions regarding War Diaries and Intelligence Summaries are contained in F.S. Regs., Part II. and the Staff Manual respectively. Title Pages will be prepared in manuscript.

8S Lanc Reg[t]
Vol 16

Place	Date	Hour	Summary of Events and Information	Remarks and references to Appendices
ROMARIN	Dec 31		Reinforcements 50 other ranks.	
DE SEULE	Jan 2/17		2nd S. Lancs relieved 8. S. Lancs at ROMARIN - 8 S. Lancs then marched to DE SEULE and took over the camp including half of CARTERS CAMP -	
	Jan 3/17		Reinforcements 1 & 8 other ranks.	
	" 6		Reinforcements 12nd Lt Beall.	
	" 7		" 78 other ranks	
	" 8		" 57 other ranks	
	" 10		" 11 other ranks	
	" 17		Went into Support at LE BIZET taking over from 8. Loyal North Lancs.	
	" 22		Took over from the 2nd S. Lancs in the front line, Battalion being DESPIERRE F.M.	
	" 29		Draft of 41 other ranks. 2nd S. Lancs relieved us in the front line, we moved to PONT DE NIEPPE.	
	" 31		In billets at PONT DE NIEPPE -	

DGNwarren
Lt. Col.
Commdg. 8 S. Lancs R[egt]
1.2.17

10102
16A

WAR DIARY or INTELLIGENCE SUMMARY

Army Form C. 2118.

8th South Lancs Regt

FEBRUARY 1917.

Place	Date	Hour	Summary of Events and Information	Remarks and references to Appendices
In the Field	1917			
	5 Feby		The Battalion left PONT DE NIEPPE & relieved 2nd South Lancs in the line LEFT LE TOUQUET SECTOR	
	" 8		were relieved in the line by 2nd South Lancs & returned to PONT DE NIEPPE.	
	" 12		relieved the 2nd South Lancs Regt in the line LEFT LE TOUQUET TRENCHES	
	" 15		were relieved by 2nd South Lancs Regt and returned to PONT DE NIEPPE.	
	" 18		Carried out a minor operation against the German trenches S.E. of PLOEGSTEERT. Casualties ※ 5 Killed and ※ 35 wounded. 3 unknown	MM 1 St EB 3
	" 20		relieved the 2nd South Lancs Regt in the line LEFT LE TOUQUET SECTOR	
	" 25		were relieved by 1st AUCKLAND REGT and returned to ROMARIN CAMP.	
	" 26		left ROMARIN CAMP and proceeded to EECKE.	

※ Includes 1 Officer Killed
2 " wounded.

Lt Colonel
8th South Lancs Regt
Commanding 8th South Lancs Regt

WAR DIARY
or
INTELLIGENCE SUMMARY

(Erase heading not required.)

Army Form C. 2118.

8 Staffs
Vol 18

Place	Date	Hour	Summary of Events and Information	Remarks and references to Appendices
EECKE	1.3.17		Whole day devoted to training of Specialists.	
	2.3.17		Training of Specialists continued, remainder employed in gun & rifle cleaning	
	3.3.17		Route march for the whole of the Battalion except B Coy.	
	4.3.17		Church service at EECKE. In the afternoon a GAS DEMONSTRATION was given by the Divisional Gas Officer.	
	5.3.17		Route march for whole of Battalion to training area where training was carried out in platoons by attack initially into extended formation.	
	6.3.17		Route march followed by attack practice from fences by sections.	
	7.3.17		The Battalion carried out training in attack after marching to ST. SYLVESTRE - CAPPEL area.	
	9.3.17		The day was spent in Physical Training, Musketry and Bayonet Practice.	
	9.3.17		Brigade marched from Godeswaersvelde Church to the Belgian frontier on practice of advance Guard formation.	
	10.3.17		Battalion & Brigade Training area.	
	11.3.17		Church Parade. Officers and N.C.O.'s trained in marching by compass.	
WARDRECQUES	12.3.17		The Battalion marched to the WESTBECOURT area, halting for the night at WARDRECQUES.	
	13.3.17		The march to the WESTBECOURT area was continued, the Battalion billeting at QUERCAMP.	
QUERCAMP	14.3.17		The day devoted to improvement of billets.	
	15.3.17		Training was carried out in billet area and on the rifle range.	
	16.3.17		The Battalion marched to Brigade training area and practised attack by companies. On return a combined attack was made on BOISINGHEM village	

Army Form C. 2118.

WAR DIARY
or
INTELLIGENCE SUMMARY
(Erase heading not required.)

Instructions regarding War Diaries and Intelligence Summaries are contained in F. S. Regs., Part II. and the Staff Manual respectively. Title Pages will be prepared in manuscript.

Place	Date	Hour	Summary of Events and Information	Remarks and references to Appendices
QUERCAMP	15.3.17		Showers were carried out in billet area and on the Rifle Range	
	16.3.17		The Battalion marched to Brigade Grounds there and practised attack in Companies. On return a combined attack was made on Rubinghen village.	
	17.3.17		Training in billets	
	18.3.17		Divine Service	
	19.3.17		Training of Specialists in billet area.	
ZUDAUSQUES	20.3.17		The Battalion left QUERCAMP and marched to ZUDAUSQUES, where a halt was made and troops billeted for the night.	
LYNDE	21.3.17		The march was continued to LYNDE.	
LE PETIT SEC BOIS	22.3.17		The Battalion made a further march to LE BORRE then halted at LE PETIT SEC BOIS.	
	23.3.17		Spent in cleaning up billets, and spent	
	24.3.17		The Battalion left LE PETIT SEC BOIS and proceeded to OUTTERSTEENE area.	
	25.3.17 31.3.17		Battalion training carried on —	

[signature]
Lt. Col.

Army Form C. 2118.

WAR DIARY
or
INTELLIGENCE SUMMARY.
(Erase heading not required.)

8 Rine Reg¹
Vol 19

19A

Place	Date	Hour	Summary of Events and Information	Remarks and references to Appendices
	APRIL			
OUTTER- STEENE	1.		In rest. Third round of Brigade football competition. A Company defeated D Company	
	2.		1/2nd S. Lancs., 5-1.	
			Battalion sports in the afternoon, but short by heavy fall of snow at 2.0 pm.	
	3.		Semi-final. A Coy defeated 75th M.G. Coy., 3-1.	
	5.		Marched to NEUVE EGLISE.	
NEUVE EGLISE.	6.		Working parties sent up to the trenches. 2nd Lieuts. W.F. FOSTER, F BUCKLER and W.F. WATSON reported for duty.	
	7.		" "	
	8.		" "	
	9.		" "	
	10.		" "	
	11.		" "	
	12.		" "	
	13.		Captain N.L. ROSS (wounded Aug. 1916) rejoined from England. Moved to BULFORD CAMP, on the road from NEUVE EGLISE to STEENWERCK.	
BULFORD CAMP	14.		Working parties and specialist training.	
	15.		" "	
	16.		Battalion Concert in the evening	

Army Form C. 2118.

WAR DIARY
or
INTELLIGENCE SUMMARY
(Erase heading not required.)

Instructions regarding War Diaries and Intelligence Summaries are contained in F. S. Regs., Part II. and the Staff Manual respectively. Title Pages will be prepared in manuscript.

Place	Date	Hour	Summary of Events and Information	Remarks and references to Appendices
BULFORD CAMP	17		Daily working parties continued. Lieut. B.M. GREEN (invalided to England Aug. 1916) reported for duty.	
	18		Working parties.	
JESUS CAMP	19		Moved to JESUS CAMP near STEENWERCK in the afternoon.	
	20		Daily working parties continued.	
	21		" "	
STRAZEELE	22		Marched to STRAZEELE.	
ST. MARIE CAPPEL	23		Marched to ST MARIE CAPPEL near CASSEL.	
	24		2/Lt. J.W. PRYOR (wounded July 1916) reported for duty.	
	25		Musketry + Bayonet fighting course, 25th Division	
	26			
	27			
	28		Capt. C.W. THEVENARD reported for duty.	
	29			
	30		Marched to OUTTERSTEENE	

J.W. Welch
Lt. Colonel
Commanding 8th ... R.
30.4.17

May to July 1917.

8th S. Lancs. Regt.

4/5/35

Army Form C. 2118

WAR DIARY
or
INTELLIGENCE SUMMARY
(Erase heading not required.)

88 Field Coy RE

Vol 20

Place	Date MAY	Hour	Summary of Events and Information	Remarks and references to Appendices
OUTTER-STEENE	1.		Training under Company arrangements.	
	2.		" " " " "	
	3.		2nd ½ Bn. Football Competition. 11th Cheshires 1, — 8th S.Lancs 1.	
	4.		Training under Company arrangements.	
	5.		Brigade Cross-country race in the afternoon won by 11th Cheshires	
	6.		Final of Football Competition replayed. 11th Cheshires 4, — 8th S.Lancs N.L.	
	7.		Brigade attack scheme on Mont de Lille.	
	9.		Battalion outlying working parties	
STEEN-WERCK.	10.		Battalion moved to CABARET du SAULE area, near STEENWERCK.	
	11. to 15.		{ Nothing particular.	
LA CRÈCHE	15.		75th Bde moved into Close billets in LA CRÈCHE.	
	16.		{ Training under company arrangements	
	20.		{	
	21.		Brigade attack scheme on Mont de Lille.	
	22.			
	23.		Working parties. A and D Companies detached, and in bivouacs near	
	24.		NEUVE EGLISE; working on battery positions	

1875. Wt. W593/826 1,000,000 4/15 J.B.C. & A. A.D.S.S./Forms/C. 2118.

Army Form C. 2118

WAR DIARY
or
INTELLIGENCE SUMMARY
(Erase heading not required.)

Instructions regarding War Diaries and Intelligence Summaries are contained in F.S. Regs., Part II. and the Staff Manual respectively. Title Pages will be prepared in manuscript.

Place	Date	Hour	Summary of Events and Information	Remarks and references to Appendices
LA CRÈCHE	25		} Working parties	
	26			
	27			
	28		Brigade scheme on Mont de Lille.	
RAVELS- BURG	29.		Brigade moved into Camp at RAVELSBURG, west of NEUVE EGLISE.	
	30.		Training under company arrangements.	
	31.		Battalion attack scheme on Mont de Lille.	
	1.		Officer Reinforcements	
	7.		2/Lr. B. HARRIS (wounded Oct. 1916)	
			2/Lr. S.T. JONES (wounded Aug. 1916)	
			Capt. C.R. CHAMBERS (wounded July 1916)	
	27.		Strength of Battalion on 31st, 40 officers, 949 other ranks.	

[signature]
Commanding 6th Bn. South Wales Bord.
31.5.17.

Army Form C. 2118

8th Sussex Regt

Vol 21

WAR DIARY
or
INTELLIGENCE SUMMARY

(Erase heading not required.)

Instructions regarding War Diaries and Intelligence Summaries are contained in F.S. Regs., Part II. and the Staff Manual respectively. Title Pages will be prepared in manuscript.

Place	Date	Hour	Summary of Events and Information	Remarks and references to Appendices
NEUVE EGLISE	1.6.17		Bn in camp at RAVELSBURG CAMP.	
"	3.6.17		Bn moved into huvacs at "Pioneer Camp. T.I.C	
"	4.6.17 5.6.17 6.6.17		WORKING PARTIES up the line	
WULVERGHEM	6.6.17	9.30p.m.	Bn moved in Assembly trenches "CRESCENT TRENCH"	
"	7.6.17 8.6.17		Attack MESSINES RIDGE between "MESSINES and WYTSCHAETE" Casualties during operations. OFFICERS { Killed 1, Wounded 6, Missing — } O.Rs { Killed 25, Wounded 118, Missing 16 }	
NEUVE EGLISE	9.6.17		Bn relieved in the Black Line by the 7th Bde, returning to rest in camp at Neuve Eglise	
	10.6.17		Proceeded Training at HILLSIDE CAMP.	

1875 Wt. W593/826 1,000,000 4/15 J.B.C. & A. A.D.S.S./Forms/C. 2118.

Army Form C. 2118

WAR DIARY
or
INTELLIGENCE SUMMARY
(Erase heading not required.)

Instructions regarding War Diaries and Intelligence Summaries are contained in F.S. Regs., Part II. and the Staff Manual respectively. Title Pages will be prepared in manuscript.

Place	Date	Hour	Summary of Events and Information	Remarks and references to Appendices
	11.6.17		Review by Corps Commander (II ANZAC). Baths.	
	12.6.17		Brig. relieves "Auckland" Batt. 4th Australian Div. in front line. Night spent in patrol work.	
	13.6.17		Enemy shelled with great intensity our front system trenches from 7pm till 10.15 pm placing in a great position freshly dug trenches and burying a number of our men. Casualties about 34 killed and wounded including Capt. Boyle O.C. "D" coy killed.	
	14.6.17		Companies were withdrawn and allotted their assembly trenches (in support) by 6.30 pm when they remained until the Artillery had quietened down with the exception of "B" coy which advanced into the forward trench vacated by the 3rd Shire soon after the opening of the barrage. This trench they consolidated and deepened. The 2nd Batt. attacked and captured STEIGNAST Fm. When Artillery had quietened moving parties were sent to Thames positions newly captured the 2nd S. Lanc. It was impossible to gain the same before daybreak owing to	

WAR DIARY
or
INTELLIGENCE SUMMARY

(Erase heading not required.)

Army Form C. 2118

Place	Date	Hour	Summary of Events and Information	Remarks and references to Appendices
	15.6.17		The latrines with which the camp from the dump. Heavy shelling of our lines, enemy aircraft flew over dropping 6 bombs in the camp. "B" relieved the 2nd Chains Regt in the front line successfully after the bombardment had ceased. No enemy to contact. It was impossible to start till 11.45 p.m.	
	16.6.17		Shelling fair, Quiet until 8 p.m. when enemy put up a heavy MG & rifle barrage. Patrols pushed between our left flank (Chess Horse) and the form Douve but found nothing except a moving car or two. MGs & Butts. Consolidation and wiring carried out on whole front.	
	17.6.17		Three coys. In front Line - B in support. General relieved fairly quiet - shell fire at intervals, dusk and after undergoing fatigue of 17/18 "B" relieved by Royal Irish Rifles and go to Pioneer Camp. N. Dranoutre.	

Place	Date	Hour	Summary of Events and Information	Remarks and references to Appendices
	18.6.17		NEUVE-EGLISE RD. B Coy caught by gas shells on way out. Three casualties.	
	19.6.17		Bn rest and batt. Programme. Parade under Coy arrangements. Recreation.	
	20.6.17		Batt. "Route march" 10 a.m. Afternoon Inter-Platoon football matches.	
	21.6.17		PARADES under Coy arrangements. Working party up the line dug new "Support line" heavily shelled resulting in 5 casualties. Party was 250 O.Rs and 6 Officers strong. Football contest continued.	
	22.6.17		Batt. Inspection Parade 3 p.m. Semi-final football comp. A company (3 Platoons) won Final of football comp.	
	23.6.17		Drill parade at 10 a.m. under Company arrangements. Inspection parade for A, B & C Companies by the Commanding Officer at 3 p.m. 10 p.m. the Battalion left NEUVE-EGLISE (Pioneer Camp) and commenced the march to the BONY area.	

Army Form C. 2118

WAR DIARY
or
INTELLIGENCE SUMMARY
(Erase heading not required.)

Place	Date	Hour	Summary of Events and Information	Remarks and references to Appendices
	24/3/17	2 am	The Battalion halted in PETIT-BOIS-SEC and rested in billets during the day.	
		11 pm	The Battalion continued its march joining the Brigade as leading battalion in AEOF DE VIEUX BERQUIN	
	25/3/17	2 am	The Battalion again halted in LE SART (MERVILLE area) and rested in billets for the day.	
		10.30 pm	March continued joining the Brigade again as leading battalion at ST VENANT. Raining hard on the march	
	26/3/17	5 am	Battalion arrived in NORRENT FONTES and halted for the day in billets.	
		11.45 pm	March resumed joining the Brigade at ST HILAIRE No 1 as rear battalion. Weather very much better.	
	27/3/17	4.30 am	Battalion arrived in BOMY and was billeted at BEAUMETZ-lès-AIRE. B Company only in proper billets	
		4 pm	B Company move to the proper billets which have been left by reinforcements for 2/5 S Divison.	
	28/3/17	9-12 (noon) 1 pm 4 pm	General cleaning up & organization of men who Battn. for the walk at MATRINGHEM, would supervision of 2/Lt PARKES	

Army Form C. 2118

WAR DIARY
or
INTELLIGENCE SUMMARY
(Erase heading not required.)

Instructions regarding War Diaries and Intelligence Summaries are contained in F.S. Regs., Part II. and the Staff Manual respectively. Title Pages will be prepared in manuscript.

Place	Date	Hour	Summary of Events and Information	Remarks and references to Appendices
BEAUMETZ les AIRE	28/6/17	2pm	Inspection of all Officers by II Corps Commander at BOMY.	
"	"	4		
"	29/6/17	7.30 am	Physical Training	
"	"	9.12.30	Battalion Training (Musketry, Bayonet fighting, Bombing)	
"	"	2.4 pm	Specialist Training	
"	30/6/17	9.30 am	Tactical Scheme "B" company on Advance guard. Battalion returned to billets before scheme was completed owing to very heavy rain.	
"	"	4 pm	Lecture by the Brigadier. Subject: "Points learnt on recent Operations"	
"	"	6.30 pm	Lecture by Pte. Foster on "Stoke's Mortars". Both Lectures were held in the School Room.	

J. M. Cook
Lieut. Colonel
Commdg. 6 "South Lancs. Regt.
1.7.17.

8th BATTALION SOUTH LANCS REGIMENT.
REPORT ON OPERATIONS 6th/10th JUNE 1917.

June 6th.

In accordance with Operation Orders, the Battalion under the Command of Major E.R.S. PRIOR M.C. moved off from the forward area camp at T.1.d. at 9.30 p.m. to take up its position in the Assembly Formation at CRESCENT TRENCH. On arriving in the vicinity of the Assembly Trench, the Battalion came under the enemy artillery fire and lost one Lewis Gun and several men on filing into the trench.

June 7th/8th.

Whilst in the Assembly Trench, the Battalion was subject to lachrymatory shells, and for most of the time every one had to wear his box-respirator, but there were no casualties.

At Zero hour plus 45 minutes, the Battalion commenced its advance passing through 7th & 74th Brigades at its appointed hours. 'A', 'B', & 'D' Companies then captured their objective on the BLACK LINE pushing out patrols which enabled them to capture 4 machine guns and numerous prisoners.

Two hours later 'C' Company advancing in conjunction with 36th Division, captured the remaining portion of the BLACK LINE. This Company was held up by machine gun fire from LUMM FARM, which was eventually assaulted and captured, taking two machine guns, one minnenwerfer and more prisoners. Lewis Guns were pushed out well in front of the position which was then consolidated and wired. The Battalion was subject to very heavy shell fire on several occasions. During the operation the Battalion sustained the following casualties:-

Officers. Killed 1.
           Wounded 6.

Other Ranks.
           Killed 21.
           Wounded 108
           Missing. 19.

June 9th.

In the early hours the Battalion was relieved by the 3rd Worcesters, and returned to rest in the neighbourhood of NEUVE EGLISE.

(see over)

(Continuation).

The following is a list of Officers who took part in the Operations with this Battalion:-

Commanding Officer. - Major E.R.S.PRIOR M.C.
Adjutant. - Lieut. J.R.BEALL.
Company Commanders.
   'A' Coy. - Capt. N.L.ROSS.
   'B' " - A/Capt. W.H.KEMBER.
   'C' " - 2nd Lt. W.F.BRYDEN.M.C.
   'D' " - A/Capt.G.CASE.

Subalterns.
- 2nd Lt. J.E.H.HILL.
- 2nd Lt. J.W.PRYOR.
- 2nd Lt. D.H.WILKINSON.
- 2nd Lt. H.J.WENN.
- 2nd Lt. B.HARRIS.
- 2nd Lt. F.BUCKLER.
- 2nd Lt. T.B.STOWELL.
- 2nd Lt. E.J.SOLOMON.
- 2nd Lt. E.G.MARSHALL.
- 2nd Lt. S.H.PARKES.
- 2nd Lt. H.S.COPPOCK.
- 2nd Lt. A.G.TICEHURST.

Signal Officer. - 2nd Lt. S.P.WILSON.

Bombing Officer. - 2nd Lt. H.FENTON.

Transport Officer. - 2nd Lt. G.M.WALTON.

Quartermaster. - Lt. & Q.M. D.DUDMAN.

Brigade Signals. - 2nd Lt. H.W.MARSDEN.

Medical Officer. - Capt E. TALBOT. (R.A.M.C.)

Liason Officers. - Lt.Col J.B.ALLSOPP
                    Capt. C.R.CHAMBERS. M.C.

Attached are names of Officers killed or wounded during the Operations.

Killed - A/Capt. W.H.KEMBER.
Wounded - 2nd Lt. S.P.WILSON.
          2nd Lt. H.W.MARSDEN.
          2nd Lt. J.E.H.HILL.
          2nd Lt. D.H.WILKINSON. (Shell shock)
          2nd Lt. H.J.WENN.
          2nd Lt. F.BUCKLER.

                                      Captain & Adjutant.
                                            for Lt.Col.
                            Commanding 8th South Lancs Regmnt.

46/25

8 McM...

WE 22

WAR DIARY
or
INTELLIGENCE SUMMARY
(Erase heading not required.)

Army Form C. 2118

Instructions regarding War Diaries and Intelligence Summaries are contained in F.S. Regs., Part II. and the Staff Manual respectively. Title Pages will be prepared in manuscript.

Place	Date	Hour	Summary of Events and Information	Remarks and references to Appendices
BEAUMETZ les AIRE	1/7/17		Church Service.	
"	1/7/17	2.30pm	Football match against 13th Cheshires which was the 1st round in the Divisional competition. Resulted in a win for the Cheshires by 4 to 3 goals.	
"	2/7/17 3/7/17		Battalion training.	
"			Battalion fired on the long range two companies in the morning and two companies in the afternoon. Staff ride at CHHEM for C.O's Adjutants and Company Commanders.	
"	4/7/17	2.30pm	Brigade Field day. The Battalion marched to practise area but owing to the weather the exercise was put off.	
"		6.15pm	Lecture in the evening on "Trench Mortars".	
"	5/7/17		Brigade Field Day in the morning and one in the afternoon. The Battalion was held in Brigade reserve.	
"	6/7/17		Battalion training.	
"		6.15pm	Lecture on "Reports & Reconnaissance" by Captain Reade. M.C.	
"		8pm	272 CHARLOT & 278 PRIE joined from ENGLAND and were posted to B & D coys respectively. Battalion made arrangements to march to MATRINGHEN	
"	7/7/17		The Battalion left BEAUMETZ les Aire by train for YPRES via to join the I Corps, 5th Army, and ... at STEENBECQUE, arriving in billets at 4 pm.	34 22

1875 Wt. W593/826 1,000,000 4/15 J.B.C. & A. A.D.S.S./Forms/C. 2118.

WAR DIARY
or
INTELLIGENCE SUMMARY
(Erase heading not required.)

Army Form C. 2118

Place	Date	Hour	Summary of Events and Information	Remarks and references to Appendices
	9/9/17	9.45am	The Battalion continued the move by bus from STEENBECQUE arriving at POPERINGHE about 1.30 pm where it debussed and marched to its destination, and were settled by 4pm in camp "DOMINION CAMP" on BUSSEBOOM area.	
	10/9/17		In the morning inspection by Companies and working parties at night to the trenches. Captain A. READE, M.C. so attached to the 8th Border regiment as 2nd in command.	
	11/9/17	11.30pm	Two Offrs (2Lt FOULKES) and 171 O.R. reported for duty. Parades under Coy arrangements. Working parties at night to the line. Casualties: O.Rs killed 1, missing 2, Wounded 2.	
	11/9/17		Working parties to the line carrying ammunition. Casualties: 2 O.Rs wounded.	
	12/9/17		Baths at HALIFAX CAMP. Working parties as usual. Casualties: shell shock 1, wounded 2 O.Rs	
	13/9/17		Working parties as usual. Casualties 2 O.Rs wounded.	
	14/9/17			

WAR DIARY or INTELLIGENCE SUMMARY

Army Form C. 2118

Place	Date	Hour	Summary of Events and Information	Remarks and references to Appendices
	15.7.17		Working parties to the Lines. "B" coy move from "Dominion" Camp to "SWAN" to "CHATEAU"	
	16.7.17		Working parties continued. Casualties heavy. 2/Lt WILKINSON wounded, 2 O.R's killed, 3 " died of wounds, 22 " wounded	
			Baths at HALIFAX Camp.	
	17.7.17		Baths continued. Also working parties. 4 Lt. this evening. 2 O.R's wounded.	
	18.7.17		Working parties continue. O.R's 10 wounded. Demonstration by Lewis gunners at WINNIPEG Camp on YUKON packs. 1 man per platoon + C.Q.M. S.s. and officers attend. "A" & "B" Coys: move up to SWAN CHATEAU for working parties.	

Army Form C. 2118

WAR DIARY
or
INTELLIGENCE SUMMARY
(Erase heading not required.)

Instructions regarding War Diaries and Intelligence Summaries are contained in F. S. Regs., Part II. and the Staff Manual respectively. Title Pages will be prepared in manuscript.

Place	Date	Hour	Summary of Events and Information	Remarks and references to Appendices
	19.7.17		Usual working parties up the line. Mr Caughlen	
	20.7.17			
	21.7.17		Again working parties.	
	22.7.17		Attend service. Battalion Less working parties head to PENINGHELST STAGING AREA "A" Owing to Divison Comdt. w.r. p.m. Working parties returned to new camp at 6. Completing new tasks.	1 O.R. wounded
	23.7.17		Rest and Bowsden under coy arrangements.	
	24.7.17		Parade carried on under coy arrangements and "Specialist" classes.	
	25.7.17		Training of Platoons under coy arrangements and specialist classes. Speech at lunch with O.C. and Officers by B.M. commander	

Army Form C. 2118

WAR DIARY
or
INTELLIGENCE SUMMARY
(Erase heading not required.)

Instructions regarding War Diaries and Intelligence
Summaries are contained in F. S. Regs., Part II.
and the Staff Manual respectively. Title Pages
will be prepared in manuscript.

Place	Date	Hour	Summary of Events and Information	Remarks and references to Appendices
	25.7.17		S.O. saw hey coy attended address by Archbishop of York at Bde Hqs	
	26.7.17		Training of platoons & Specialists continued in morning. In aft. Batt. Sports and Batt. concert in evening.	
	27.7.17		Baths at "Hoopoutre". C.O's inspection of coys' readiness for next active operations.	
	28.7.17		Army Commander ~~visited~~ visits camp with Div. General. Johnson Service.	
	29.7.17		Training under Company arrangements 9 A.M.— 12 noon. Lecture by Commanding officer to all officers 2 P.M.	
	30.7.17		Battalion move to Assembly position at BELGIAN CHATEAU. AREA at 10 P.M. ready for offensive action.	

for O.C. 8. South Wales Bord.
- 8.17

WAR DIARY or INTELLIGENCE SUMMARY

Army Form C. 2118

Place	Date	Hour	Summary of Events and Information	Remarks and references to Appendices
WESTHOEK RIDGE	1/8/17	12 midday	This afternoon while reconnoitering the front line previous to moving to the Battalion, Lieut-Col Ablanff was wounded in the back by shell splinter and proceeded to the base this evening. At 2 pm D & A Coys moved up into support during relief. The enemy counter attacked on the immediate objective the YPRES-ROULERS RLY., driving out the 2nd Middlesex Regt. D.Y. of the 8th L.N.L. Regt. under Lieut. Romans repulsed the enemy and moved up so as to occupy the approximate position previously held by the Middlesex during operation. It was greatly assisted by the Camerons who attacked from the left flank. All 8 pm the remainder of the Battalion moved up to complete the relief of the sector then held by the 2nd Devons, and Capt. Colquhoun took command of the Battalion temporarily.	23
WESTHOEK RIDGE	2/8/17	12 p.m.	Major Brown arrived at 6 am this morning to take command of the Battalion. Owing to the day misting unusual occurred but the enemy fitfully shelled Q.M. Stanwick and the approach from Ypres in Potijze & Stunnick.	
ditto	3/8/17	12 p.m.	Casualties amongst the rank & file were 8 killed 29 wounded. Enemy continued to shell us heavily all day and obtained several direct hits on my Battalion Headquarters (which Lost I to be evacuated at about 5·30 pm) and Potijze House adjoining.	23 A

Casualties: Officers Killed (Lt. Roman) 2nd Lieut. ...
Lt. Rainer 2/Lt. Bayley Lt. Col. Ablanff wounded, also

1875 Wt. W593/826 1,000,000 4/15 I.B.C. & A. A.D.S.S./Forms/C. 2118.

WAR DIARY or INTELLIGENCE SUMMARY

Army Form C. 2118

(Erase heading not required.)

Place	Date	Hour	Summary of Events and Information	Remarks and references to Appendices
TEETHER RIDGE	4/8/17	12 p.m.	Heavily shelled by enemy, otherwise situation normal. Casualties 3 killed 25 wounded	
"	5/8/17	12 p.m.	Quiet.	
"	6/8/17	12 p.m.	Nothing unusual happened during the day shelling by enemy not so persistent. Casualties 9 killed 32 wounded.	
YPRES	7/8/17	12 p.m.	At 1 p.m. the enemy put a heavy barrage down the whole length of the line, we retired in the Battalion moved back in the Infantry Barracks YPRES at about 3 am this morning and they will report in morning. Casualties 5 killed 28 wounded.	
RAILWAY WOOD	8/8/17	12 p.m.	At 6 p.m. the Battalion moved up to RAILWAY HOUSE from where we retired & immediately moved again to RAILWAY WOOD to support the 14th Brigade who went to attack at about 11-30 p.m. this evening.	
HALIFAX CAMP	9/8/17	12 p.m.	We returned from Railway Wood to Halifax forest about 3 am this morning, the attack by the 14th Brigade having been punctured, at 2-30 p.m. we started back for HALIFAX CAMP where we arrived about 4 p.m. without casualty.	
"	10/8/17	12 p.m.	The day has been spent in refitting and re-equipping about 4 p.m. this morning an enemy aeroplane bombed the camp area. The Battalion had no casualties.	
WESTHOEK RIDGE	11/8/17	12 p.m.	We arrived here at 3 p.m. the front line at 10-30 p.m. having been called upon from HALIFAX CAMP to relieve the 1/4 Lancashire Fusiliers who had suffered heavy casualties.	
"	12/8/17	12 p.m.	We have held the line without any further unusual .... except that one of the machine guns attached to this event was knocked out & .... artillery and two killed.	

WAR DIARY or INTELLIGENCE SUMMARY

Army Form C. 2118

Place	Date	Hour	Summary of Events and Information	Remarks and references to Appendices
WESTHOEK RIDGE	15/8/17	12 p.m.	We continued to hold the line here. The enemy shelled all Company Headquarters very heavily intermittently and put up S.O.S. at 9.15 p.m. then every ½ hour which followed well up own relief. We heard rifles for a short time but they succeeded in getting through without a single casualty. Lieut. Honey was killed and 2/Lt. Parker severely wounded by direct hit on D Coy Hd. Qtrs. 2/Lt. Bagley was also wounded by shrapnel while holding post in front line.	
DOMINION CAMP	14/8/17	12 p.m.	The Battalion arrived here early this morning from the line, without suffering any casualties during the journey.	
	W. 15/8/17		Rained heavily. In similar portion of the day Capt. H. Rose returned from 8th Battalion to assist & up relief of 2nd in Command. Men spent time cleaning equipment. Reinforcement numbering 54 other ranks joined Battn. today 9 were posted to "D" Coy.	
YPRES	Th. 16/8/17		Showery. Battn. moved from DOMINION CAMP to the RAMPARTS – YPRES. During my is carrying party of 200 provided to assist in making forward dump & water arrangement by 8th Divn. (casuals nil)	
	F. 17/8/17		Fine. Relieved from RAMPARTS – YPRES by 19th London Regt. at 7:30 p.m. Battn. arrived at VLAMERTINGHE and detrained at EECKE.	
EECKE AREA	Sat 18/8/17		Fine. Battn. arrived at billets at 4 a.m. Men rested during day & cleaned equipment.	

Army Form C. 2118

WAR DIARY
or
INTELLIGENCE SUMMARY
(Erase heading not required.)

Instructions regarding War Diaries and Intelligence Summaries are contained in F.S. Regs., Part II. and the Staff Manual respectively. Title Pages will be prepared in manuscript.

Place	Date	Hour	Summary of Events and Information	Remarks and references to Appendices
EECKE AREA.	S. 19/8/17		Fine. Church parades during morning. During afternoon all deficiencies taken. Divnl Genl called at B.H.Q. to make enquiries re billets & general comfort of the men. Lt. Foulkes proceeded to no 1. Camp & Lt. Fendon proceeded on leave today.	
STEENVOORDE AREA.	M. 20/8/17.		Fine. Batt.n moved from EECKE AREA to STEENVOORDE AREA. The move was completed by noon. Lt. Green rejoined from hospital. Reinforcements 84 Other ranks — arrived today.	
	T. 21/8/17.		Fine. The Brigade was today inspected by the Commander in Chief & marched past in column of Platoon.	
	W. 22/8/17.	10.10 a.m.	Fine – Batt.n training. Remainder parade 8-30 to 9-30. Physical training 9-30 to 10.30. Special classes of instruction 10-30 to 12-30. Remainder musketry. Bayonet fighting – extended order drill. During afternoon recreational training.	
	Th. 23/8/17.		Fine. Training as on previous day. Capt. Beall & Lt Bay have proceeded on 5 days leave to PARIS. Hd. Qrs. despatched B.Coy. at Footbll 3 – 2.	
	F. 24/8/17		Showery. Battalion marched to ranges at ST. MARIE - CAPPEL and all men fired three practices (1) Grouping (2) Classification (3) application. Lt. Fielding proceeded on leave today.	
	Sat. 25/8/17.	10-12.30	Fine. Batt.n training. 8-30 to 9-30 Ceremonial parade. 9-30 to 10 a.m. Physical training. Special classes of instruction. Remainder musketry & bayonet fighting. In the afternoon a lecture on Hygiene was given by Capt Ballard on "following reinforcement" arrived to-day.	

1875 Wt. W593/826 1,000,000 4/15 J.B.C. & A. A.D.S.S./Forms/C. 2118.

Army Form C. 2118

WAR DIARY
or
INTELLIGENCE SUMMARY
(Erase heading not required.)

Instructions regarding War Diaries and Intelligence Summaries are contained in F. S. Regs., Part II. and the Staff Manual respectively. Title Pages will be prepared in manuscript.

Place	Date	Hour	Summary of Events and Information	Remarks and references to Appendices
STEENVOORDE AREA	S. 26/8/17		Reinforcements — 2/Lt. Wenn (wounded 7/6/17 - rejoined 1st duty.) Lt/Sgt. Cullen, 21 other ranks. Major Prior today takes the rest of the F.M. which commanded by the Battⁿ. Fine. Church parades during morning. Lewis gun classes gun instructors continued as on previous days.	
	M. 27/8/17		Fine. Battⁿ parade 8-30 to 9-30. Specialist classes 9-30 to 12-30. Remainder mustering & bayonet fighting. During afternoon inter-company football matches. In evening treat given to all men engaged in Brigade Sports.	
	T. 28/8/17		Rain in morning stopped during afternoon. Brigade Sports postponed owing to weather conditions. Training as on previous day. 2000 Battⁿ to baths.	
	W. 29/8/17		Showery. Training as on Monday. Brigade Sports held during afternoon. Battⁿ did remarkably well taking no fewer than three firsts and eleven seconds in the events.	
	Th. 30/8/17		Fine. Battⁿ parade 8-30 to 9-30. Spreadeagle 9-30 to 12-30. Remainder mustering & do drill musketry. During afternoon Battⁿ football team played 8th Border Regt & defeated them 4–2. In evening Brigade Boxing Competition. Competitors from Battⁿ won two events, one of the final.	

1875 Wt. W593/826 1,000,000 4/15 I.B.C. & A. A.D.S.S./Forms/C. 2118.

Army Form C. 2118.

WAR DIARY
or
INTELLIGENCE SUMMARY.
(Erase heading not required.)

Place	Date	Hour	Summary of Events and Information	Remarks and references to Appendices
STEENVOORDE AREA	31/8/17		Zinn. Batt⁰ parade 8·30 to 9·30. Sp'wunder's class 9·30 to 12·30. All rifle grenadiers Lewis gunners First Aid & rifle grenadiers. Remainder of Batt⁰ musketry, physical training, bayonet fighting. During afternoon Batt⁰ going to 2ⁿᵈ Bomb fences at cricket. Results — 2ⁿᵈ Batt⁰ 65 — 8ᵗʰ Batt⁰ 33. Baths at Wardrecques available this morning 250.	

Signed/ A. Roland.
Commdg. 6ᵗʰ Bn. Suth. Lancs. R.
31. B. M.

Army Form C. 2118

WAR DIARY
or
INTELLIGENCE SUMMARY
(Erase heading not required.)

8 Army Tp
E.O.D.

24A

Place	Date	Hour	Summary of Events and Information	Remarks and references to Appendices
STEENVOORDE AREA	Sat 1/9/17		Showery. Batt⁴ moved at 12-40 p.m. to DEVONSHIRE CAMP arriving there at 4 p.m. 2/Lt. Mr. D. Bull in Israel invalided to England sick.	
DEVONSHIRE CAMP	Sun 2/9/17		Showery. During morning Church Parades. At 1 p.m. Batt⁴ moved to DICKEBUSCH AREA and arrived at 4 p.m. Enemy aircraft active during the night.	
DICKEBUSCH AREA	M. 3/9/17		Fine. All companies inspected by Commanding Officer - dress fighting order. During remainder of day Coy. at disposal of Coy. Commanders. At 10 p.m. two Coys. detailed for work under C.R.E. at Div⁹ Headquarters. Enemy aircraft again active during night.	
	T. 4/9/17		Fine. Parades under Coy. arrangements. Twin running parades under R.E. Officers. Two Coy⁹ again detailed for work under C.R.E. at Div⁹ Headquarters. B. team moved to MILLAM at 12-30 p.m. Major Read commanded B. team.	
	W. 5/9/17		Fine. At 6 p.m. Batt⁴ moved from DICKEBUSCH AREA to relieve 12th WILTS REGT. (7th Bde.) at ZILLEBEKE BUND. Batt⁴ in room. Relief complete at 9 p.m. No casualties.	
ZILLEBEKE BUND	Th 6/9/17		Fine. At 3-30 p.m. D. Coy provided working party of 1 Officer & 60 men to relieve 9 men at ZOUAVE TRENCH. Occasional shelling of C & D Coy's dugouts. Casualties 1 other rank wounded.	

1875 Wt. W593/826 1,000,000 4/15 J.B.C. & A. A.D.S.S./Forms/C. 2118.

WAR DIARY or INTELLIGENCE SUMMARY

Army Form C. 2118

Place	Date	Hour	Summary of Events and Information	Remarks and references to Appendices
ZILLEBEKE F. BUND.	7/9/17		Fine. Working parties on ZOUAVE TRENCH continued. 1 Officer & Bombers from each Coy detailed for show parties, starting work at 5 a.m. – 9 a.m. 12 noon & 9 p.m. respectively. No casualties. Quiet day.	
	Sat. 8/9/17		Fine. Work proceeded as yesterday. Very wet & showery. Two casualties.	
	Sun. 9/9/17		Fine during day. Work on ZOUAVE TRENCH continued under O.P. — Battn. was relieved by 8th LONDON REGT. (142 Brigade) & proceeded to DICKEBUSCH AREA (Canal Reserve Camp). At approx. midnight since left bombed. Brigade Transport lines at DICKEBUSCH. Casualties both ranks unreported.	
CANAL RESERVE CAMP.	M. 10/9/17		Fine. At noon Battn. moved to HALIFAX CAMP. Remainder of day spent cleaning equipment.	
HALIFAX CAMP.	T. 11/9/17		Fine. The whole of the day was spent in cleaning and fitting up of equipment preparatory to moving to Back area.	
	W. 12/9/17		Fine. Battn. entrained at 3-45 p.m. at HALIFAX CAMP and moved to CAESTRE AREA arriving at 3 a.m. "B" Reserve reported 13 Bn. "B" Reinforcement. W/ other ranks — 2/Lt S. Maddock, 2/Lt F. Hackwood, 2/Lt J.R. Dare, 2/Lt J. Atkinson, 2/Lt J.H. Tilley.	

WAR DIARY
INTELLIGENCE SUMMARY

Army Form C. 2118

(Erase heading not required.)

Instructions regarding War Diaries and Intelligence Summaries are contained in F.S. Regs., Part II. and the Staff Manual respectively. Title Pages will be prepared in manuscript.

Place	Date	Hour	Summary of Events and Information	Remarks and references to Appendices
CAESTRE AREA	Th. 13/9/17	6.45 a.m. – 9	Fine but cloudy. Batt'n marched to STEENBECQUE AREA starting at 6.30 a.m. arriving at 2-45 p.m. The men fell out on the march.	
STEENBECQUE AREA	F. 14/9/17		Cloudy. Batt'n marched to ALLOUAGNE AREA starting at 6.30 a.m. The area was reached at 2 p.m. The distance marched on each day was 20 Kilometres.	
ALLOUAGNE AREA	Sat. 15/9/17		Fine. The whole of the day was devoted to cleaning and inspection. Parades with Coy. arrangements. Capt. Kerr attended from 2nd Army School. 5th Corps School.	
	Sun. 16/9/17		During afternoon a vain inspection. Capt. R.C. 8.45 – 9 Non-Commissioned, 9–30. Christ Parade C.O.E. 10 a.m. R.C. 10 a.m. 5th Division went to Divisional organised Service. Capt. Kerr went to lecture on "Leave the 1st Corps School to musketry training".	
	M. 17/9/17	8.30 a.m. – 10 a.m. Batt'n parade. 9–12.30 Batt'n training – Musketry 9–12.30. Physical training bayonet fighting. Bombing. Lewis gun and civil Afternoon organised recreation. Inter-company football match D Coy 4 B Coy 2. Lt. Dennis rejoined from 2nd Army Infantry School 9 T.M. School.	
	T. 18/9/17		Showery. Training as on previous day. No opening received owing to rain.	
	W. 19/9/17		Fine. Training continued as on Monday. Organised matches part of musketry Batt'n football team of against Th. Rest. result B's 7 Rest 0. Lt. Wynn returned from Small Arms School.	
	Th. 20/9/17		Fine. Batt'n find 2 practice (rapid wire-cutting) on long range D.B.A. during month (7 a.m – 3 p.m). Allowance B's score 5 sites defence R.E. 2 – 0. Batt'n ordered to ride defended The Monmouths 6th ord. B Coy above side defended against north against from Kyomi. 11 Other ranks	

1875—Wt. W593/826 1,000,000 4/15 J.B.C. & A. A.D.S.S./Forms/C. 2118.

WAR DIARY or INTELLIGENCE SUMMARY

Army Form C. 2118

(Erase heading not required.)

Instructions regarding War Diaries and Intelligence Summaries are contained in F. S. Regs, Part II. and the Staff Manual respectively. Title Pages will be prepared in manuscript.

Place	Date	Hour	Summary of Events and Information	Remarks and references to Appendices
ALLOUAGNE AREA	Fri 21/9/17		Fine. 8-30 to 9 a.m. Bn. 1st parade. 9.10-12-30 Route march. Route taken LOZINGHEM — AUCHEL — RAIMBERT — BURBURE — ALLOUAGNE. 4th Wash. on B. Thro ranks previous on arm. Books at other ranks = 137. 160 other ranks.	
	Sat 22/9/17		8.30 - 9 A.M. Bn. parade. 9.-12.30. Training. Musketry. Bayonet fighting, Musketry. Afternoon Recreation.	
	Sun 23/9/17		10 A.M. Nov. confirmate 11.15 a.m. R.C. 8.45 a.m. Church Parade. 6. H.E. Church 10 a.m. Rev. Monmouth. Afternoon Rugby football match Y & B — 5 pts. Salvation Army 6 pts.	
	Mon 24/9/17		Fine. Training continued as on termn. Lecture at 5 p.m. by Major ABERCROMBIE G.S.O.2 10 Divn. on Recent fighting around LENS to all officers and NCOs attending.	
	Tue 25/9/17		Fine. Battalion firing practices Lewis & Nº 2 on longrange. Nº 4 shortrange. Special blanks & Lewis Gunners, Stretcher Bearers, Signallers parade in their own platoons. 6 Bn. S.H.B. Bn. Los 5pts. No. Afternoon Bn. rugby team Y. Bn. Los Shino fighting. All available officers Evening Lecture by Col.— Thomas on "Shrui fighting" NCOs attend.	
	Wed 26/9/17		Fine. Training continued as on termn. Afternoon Divisional Y.M. Battalion also marches to sports Afternoon were to supply attendants.	

Army Form C. 2118.

WAR DIARY
or
INTELLIGENCE SUMMARY.
(Erase heading not required.)

Instructions regarding War Diaries and Intelligence Summaries are contained in F.S. Regs., Part II. and the Staff Manual respectively. Title pages will be prepared in manuscript.

Place	Date	Hour	Summary of Events and Information	Remarks and references to Appendices
HUMANE AREA.	Thurs 27-9-17		Battalion moved by Bus via to Mazin and Bus Stendon Epinette in CITÉ ST. PIERRE (WEST). Time of arriving 5pm.	
CITÉ ST PIERRE	Friday 28-9-17		Battalion relieved 9th Bn. NORFOLK Regt in the front line trenches. Relief commenced at 8pm. Casualties 1 Officer (2 Lt Muller) wounded. 10 O.R. killed. 8 O.R. wounded. Disposition of Bn. C & D. Coys front line. A Coy Support B Coy reserve.	
LENS.	Saturday 29-9-17		No casualties during day. Working parties attacked up Camp. Sur observing of trenches &c.	
	Friday 30-9-17		Working parties continued as yesterday.	

(signature) Lieut Colonel
Commanding 8 South Lancs Regt.
30. 9. 17

Army Form C. 2118.

WAR DIARY
or
INTELLIGENCE SUMMARY.
(Erase heading not required.)

8th South Lancs

Instructions regarding War Diaries and Intelligence Summaries are contained in F.S. Regs., Part II. and the Staff Manual respectively. Title pages will be prepared in manuscript.

Place	Date Oct.	Hour	Summary of Events and Information	Remarks and references to Appendices
LENS Sector	M.1		Fine. Fourth day in front line. Work of improving trenches & wiring of bombing posts continued. Four patrols during night. Working of Signallers to report Capt. Bryden proceeded on leave to England.	
	T.2		Fine. Fifth day in front line. Work continued as yesterday. Four patrols during night. Enemy wire opposite CHICORY TRENCH found to be very weak and no organised shell hole in front of trench.	
	W.3		Showery. Sixth day in front line. Work continued as yesterday. No patrols.	
	Th.4		Showery. Enemy raided our trenches immediately NORTH & SOUTH of the sector held by us. The whole front was barraged. Enemy were driven by rifle & machine gun fire. B Coy was relieved at 10.30 p.m. by the 1st Shropshire Light Infantry Canadian Killed 6 wounded	
BULLY GRENAY AREA	F.5		Fine. Battalion arrived in Fields at BULLY GRENAY at 2 A.M. At 7.30 A.M. Battalion moved into Camp at HOUCHIN arriving there at 11.45 A.M.	
HOUCHIN AREA	Sat.6		Showery. Batt'n moved at 5 p.m. and relieved 2nd B'n South Lancs 5 Regt in Brigade Reserve (CANAL SECTOR - LE PREOL) Relief completed by 8 p.m.	25 F
LE PREOL	S.7		Rained heavily. Day spent in cleaning & filling of equipment.	
	M.8		Torrential rain storms. Day devoted to kit inspection by Company Majors. 'B' Coys inspection Major B' Evans visiting in Major at 1 p.m. from BETHUNE	

Army Form C. 2118.

WAR DIARY
or
INTELLIGENCE SUMMARY.
(Erase heading not required.)

Instructions regarding War Diaries and Intelligence Summaries are contained in F.S. Regs., Part II and the Staff Manual respectively. Title pages will be prepared in manuscript.

Place	Date	Hour	Summary of Events and Information	Remarks and references to Appendices
LE PREOL	T. 9.		Stormy. Parades under Coy. arrangements. All Officers reconnoitred the new sector. (CANAL SECTOR.)	
	W. 10		Heavy rain during morning. Training under Coy. arrangement. Officers again reconnoitred front line	
	Th. 11.		Stormy. Baths allotted to Bn - 410. Remainder of time training under Coy. arrangements	
	F. 12.		Stormy. Baths again allotted during morning. 2/Lt M Prior & 4 other ranks proceeded on leave. Seven reinforcements reported to us. Capt. Keit was attached to 73rd Bde. Instructional Platoon for 7th Division. Attended the same for a course of instruction. 11 OR proceeded to Corps School. Bn relieved 2nd Bn South Wales Regt in front line (CANAL LEFT SECTOR) relief commencing at 6P -
CANAL LEFT SECTOR	Sat. 13		Stormy. Work continued improving trenches, especially on extreme left. (MARLINGHAM CRATER). HQ at Coys. during the first eleven night. 2/Lt Ickenson & 2/Lt Tilley and 10 OR proceeded to II Corps School	
	S. 14.		Fine. Work on trenches continued. Patrols during night reported no movement till quiet. Wiring continued	
	M. 15.		Fine. Three O.R. proceeded to Rest Camp (Army). The work of completing STRATHCONA WALK and the element of 30 yds of underwear called in sand walk is an previous day, continued	

2353 Wt. W2514/1454 700,000 5/15 D.D.&L. A.D.S.S./Forms/C. 2118.

WAR DIARY or INTELLIGENCE SUMMARY

Army Form C. 2118

(Erase heading not required.)

Place	Date	Hour	Summary of Events and Information	Remarks and references to Appendices
CANAL LEFT SECTOR	T. 16.		Fine. Work continued on STRATHCONA WALK. Intermittent shelling during morning (minenwerfer shells) on front & support trenches north of CANAL. Casualties 4 OR killed & 2 OR wounded. Wire of wiring party cut by shell-burst previous (?) night.	
	W. 17		Fine. Enemy again range-ik on front & support lines & other posts. He was noticed with a view to making some more extensive (?) work of repair during night. 9 reported trenches shelling day. Officers & N.C.O's from each Coy reconnoitred support line.	
	Th. 18.		Fine. Six senior N.C.O. instructors attached to 2 & 1st South Staffs. Gt. Bn. were retired by 2nd Bn. South Lancs Regt. Relief completed at 3.30 pm. Bn. moved into support.	
	F. 19		Fine. Reinforcement of 5 OR reported for duty today. The Genl & 4 OR proceeded on leave. Working parties under the R.E's were furnished by all Coys.	
	Sat. 20		Fine. Working parties furnished for front line as on previous day. Capts. E.W. Thornton reported from D.R.B. for duty.	
	S. 21.		Fine. Battn. allotted to 15 Corp. Working parties furnished as on previous days. Reinforcements 2 OR. The fatigue parties on holding Canon Canadian 2.O.R.	
	M. 22.		Fine. Battn. again allotted 15 Corp. Working parties as on previous day. 6 other ranks reinforcement's.	

Army Form C. 2118

WAR DIARY
or
INTELLIGENCE SUMMARY
(Erase heading not required.)

Instructions regarding War Diaries and Intelligence Summaries are contained in F.S. Regs., Part II. and the Staff Manual respectively. Title Pages will be prepared in manuscript.

Place	Date	Hour	Summary of Events and Information	Remarks and references to Appendices
CANAL LEFT SECTOR	T.23		Fine. Working parties furnished. Working 235mm — to R.E's. Casualties 3 O.R. wounded.	
	W.24		Fine. Batt'n relieved in support by 2 Cheshires from relief relieved 2nd Bn South Lancs in front line. Relief commenced at 9.30 — & was completed by 11-30 am. Heavy shelling during day.	
	Th.25		Morning. At 4.10 a.m. enemy raided our lines on estimated strength of 40 — advanced 4 hours 12 XII. They attempted to enter our trenches at two points. They were driven off at one point by Lewis guns & rifle fire and forced back at the other point. They were supported by trench mortar & other heavy weapons. Casualties 4 other ranks wounded.	
	F.26		Rain. Owing to bombardment & damage to drains trenches on left were flooded. All available men worked on drains & trenches. By night all trenches were passable & during night most parts were redrained. No lives were lost.	
	Sat.27.		Cloudy. Work continued as on previous day. Trenches were cleaned of water & workings. During evening gas was prevalent. Skin pads evening night. G.P. stand-by's provided on Hill Cog. Signal Comn's.	
	S.28.		Fine. Everything very quiet during day. Enemy shelling was active especially during night. On relation our sight & trench.	

Army Form C. 2118

WAR DIARY
or
INTELLIGENCE SUMMARY
(Erase heading not required.)

Instructions regarding War Diaries and Intelligence Summaries are contained in F. S. Regs., Part II. and the Staff Manual respectively. Title Pages will be prepared in manuscript.

Place	Date	Hour	Summary of Events and Information	Remarks and references to Appendices
CANAL LEFT SECTOR	M. 29		Fine. Scouts were out front guide normal. Capt. & Adjt. J.P. Robb proceeded on leave today. Lt. Col. Prior rd. arrvd. from leave. 9 former Bt. in the lines. Wiring parties on trenches continued during night.	
	T. 30		Showing. Intermittent shelling during morning. Bt. was relieved in the line by 2nd Bt. South Lancs Regt. Relief commenced at 3 p. & was complete by 5 p.m. Bt. moved into Brigade Reserve at Le PREOL. Remainder of 4th A.P.P. Bde. and 2 Cos nearly reported for duty.	
	W. 31		Fine. Day spent by Coys. cleaning up equipment, clothing, etc. Were inspected in. Batts. addition 10 to 3 at 2.	

[signature]
[signature]
Lieut. Colonel
Commanding 6th Bn. South Lancs. Regt.
31.10.17.

Army Form C. 2118.

WAR DIARY
or
INTELLIGENCE SUMMARY.
(Erase heading not required.)

8' Bn. J Rowes Regt. Vol 2

Place	Date	Hour	Summary of Events and Information	Remarks and references to Appendices
LE PREOL	M.1st		Transport under Company arrangements. Specialists under their respective Officers. Baths were arranged for men (240) from 9 to 12-3075. Lecture on bombing given by Lt Edwards 5-307.	
	F.2.		Training as yesterday. Musical lecture is being given to recruits during Reinforcements, 2 other ranks.	
	S.3		Fire Batt parade by Companies for inspection by Command of Officer Capt. Davis. 9.3 other ranks proceeded on leave today. 11/Lt G.E.P. Bott reported for duty & Lieut Drummond to 8th Bn also Bgt — Remainder of day spent in usual manner.	
	Sun.4		Church parades 11 am. Strong wind.	
CANAL SECTOR	M.5.		Rain. The Bn relieved 8th Border Regt in Supports. The 3rd C.E.P. held the left sub-sector of the line for instructional purposes. Liaison officers were furnished from the Bn i.e. the Coys of the 3rd C.E.P.? Also sergeants were dealt to act as platoon Sgts when men under the orders of Majr Grieve. Lt. J.R. Dow returned from leave from Eng. care. Working parties detailed for work of improving Communication line. Capt. Turner provided on a Liaison Cover of inspection to C 110 Battery R.F.A.	26a
	T.6.			

WAR DIARY
or
INTELLIGENCE SUMMARY.
(Erase heading not required.)

Army Form C. 2118.

Place	Date	Hour	Summary of Events and Information	Remarks and references to Appendices
CANAL SECTOR.	Nov. W. 7		Fine. Working parties detailed as on previous day. 2/Lt. D. McK. Moran & 2/Lt. J.W. Patterson on reported for duty. 2nd Lt. The N.C.O. instructor & 4 O/Rs & 4 3rd South Staffords to Casualties returned from attachment to 4th/5th South Staffs. Casualties one other rank killed, one other rank died of wounds & one other rank wounded. The 4/Lt. Mr. D. Buchanan returned from leave.	
	Th. 8		Fine. Working parties detailed as on previous day. One platoon from "C" Coy. held BRICKSTACKS & one platoon of "B" (?) held CRATERS on the left Subr. sector during tour of duty of 3rd C.E.P. Capt. G.R. Kerr (attached Instruction Platoon 3rd/Bn.) & 2 other ranks wounded.	
	F. 9		Fine. 1Bn/17 relieved 3rd C.E.P. in left Subr sector. Relief was completed by 11 a.m. Cavalries oil.	
	Sat. 10		Showery. Work of improving trenches especially near CRATERS continued. POWs had nothing to report. Enemy activity nil. 2/Lt. R.H. Price & 2/Lt. E. Tredden proceeded on courses of instruction to 1st Army School. Capt. & Adjt. G.R. Brash returned from tour at Army School.	
	S. 11		Showery. Batt'n. War relieved by 2nd /9/5 South Lancs Regt. T went into support. 2/Lt. J. Ashton returned from 4th Corps. Infantry School.	

Army Form C. 2118.

WAR DIARY
or
INTELLIGENCE SUMMARY.
(Erase heading not required.)

Instructions regarding War Diaries and Intelligence Summaries are contained in F. S. Regs., Part II. and the Staff Manual respectively. Title pages will be prepared in manuscript.

Place	Date	Hour	Summary of Events and Information	Remarks and references to Appendices
CANAL SECTOR	M.12		Rain at intervals. Working parties detailed for improving Communication trenches & also for carrying material to front Line. 6 other ranks reported for duty from 25th D.R.B. Major H. Rean proceeded on leave.	
	T.13		Cloudy. Working parties as yesterday.	
	W.14		Fine. Working parties as on previous days. 2 O.R. 1 wounded. 10 Casualty Clearing Station.	
	Th.15		Fine. Lt. D.H. Paton returned from hospital went on 7 off/or Coy Nr 2. Working parties as on previous days. One other rank wounded.	
	F.16		Fine. Working parties detailed as on previous days.	
	S.17		Fine. The Batt. 1st returned 2nd Bn South Lancs Regt. in the front line. Relief was completed by 11-30 a.m. Lt. R.S. Johnson proceeded on leave. Reinforcement of one other rank.	
	Sun.18		Fine. Enemy very active during the night with minenwerfers. Casualties 4 other ranks killed and 7 wounded. Reinforcements 2 other ranks.	
	M.19		Cloudy. Enemy active with artillery continues. Patrols report enemy wiring. Lt. F.B. Stewart M.C. joined. Total of wounds received today.	

Army Form C. 2118.

WAR DIARY
or
INTELLIGENCE SUMMARY.
(Erase heading not required.)

Instructions regarding War Diaries and Intelligence Summaries are contained in F.S. Regs., Part II. and the Staff Manual respectively. Title pages will be prepared in manuscript.

Place	Date 11.17	Hour	Summary of Events and Information	Remarks and references to Appendices
CANAL SECTOR	T.20.		Fine. Enemy putra sin in No Man's Land during night. One enemy wounded & captured, the afterwards died of wounds (Rgt. - 453 R.I.R.). Casualties one other rank wounded. Capt. Harris returned from leave.	
	W.21.		Fine. Enemy less active in enemy. Reinforcements 2/Lt G.H. Hill reported for duty 1.0 p.m.	
	Th.22		Fine. Work of revetting trenches near CRATERS pushed forward. Capt. C.R. Chevalier proceeded on a six days' course of instruction to C110. Battery R.F.A. Capt. Talbot & 2/Lt L.J. Warren proceeded on leave.	
	F.23		Fine. Bn. was relieved by 2nd Bn. South Wales Rgt. Bn. moved into Reserve at LE PREOL. Relief completed by 4-30 p.m.	
LE PREOL	S.24.		Fine. The whole of the day was devoted to general cleaning up. Baths attended by (195) during the day. Small working parties also furnished. Reinforcements, 2/Lt ? Shaw, 2/Lt ? E. Mackay & 2/Lt W. Napier reported for duty.	
	Sun.25.	11 a.m.	Fine. Church Parade 11 a.m. - Working parties furnished as on previous day. Reinforcements 2/Lt E. McDiarmuid, 2/Lt F. ? & 2/Lt B.M. Grierson on previous day. 2/Lt R.T. ? returned from hospital.	

Army Form C. 2118.

WAR DIARY
or
INTELLIGENCE SUMMARY.
(Erase heading not required.)

Place	Date	Hour	Summary of Events and Information	Remarks and references to Appendices
LE PREOL	M. 26		Fine. Training under Company arrangements. Special attention is being paid to regt. workings. Capt. C.R. Gardner was today granted special leave to U.K. 2nd Lieuten. J.H. Watson proceeded on course of instruction to 1st Corps School. Major J. Rush returned from leave.	
	T. 27.		Showery. Training continued as yesterday. Ranks allotted to Coys. during day. Ten other ranks returned from attachment to 105 Field Coy. R.E.	
	W. 28		Fine. Battn. was relieved in reserve by 1/5th Bn. Lancashire Fusiliers & proceeded to FOUQUEREUIL. Lt. B.M. Green proceeded on leave. Reinforcement one other rank.	
FOUQUER-EUIL	TH 29	1 pm	Fine. Battn. marched to BURBURE arriving in billets at 1pm. Lt. Br. J.B. Allopp returned today & took over command of the Battn.	
BURBURE	F. 30		Showery. Battn. marched BEAUMETZ LES AIRES arriving at 4p.m.	

J.B. Allopp
Lt. Col.
Commanding 8th Bn. East Lancs. Regt.

Army Form C. 2118.

WAR DIARY
or
INTELLIGENCE SUMMARY.
(Erase heading not required.)

8th Bn: S. Lancs Regt.

Vol 27

Instructions regarding War Diaries and Intelligence Summaries are contained in F. S. Regs., Part II. and the Staff Manual respectively. Title pages will be prepared in manuscript.

Place	Date Dec	Hour	Summary of Events and Information	Remarks and references to Appendices
BEAUMETZ -LEZ- AIRE	S.1		Fine. The rest of the day devoted to general cleaning up of clothing. 2nd. W.G. Nettleh was admitted to hospital.	
	Sun.2		Fine. Church Parade. Coys. C. & R.C. All billets were inspected by Commanding Officer.	
	M.3		Fine. Battalion proceeded by march route and train to 3rd Army Area. Entraining station ANVIN. Detraining station ACHIET LE GRAND. Battalion entrained at 8.20 p.m.	
GOMIECOURT CAMP			Fine. Battalion arrived at ACHIET-LE-GRAND at 7 a.m. & marched to GOMIECOURT CAMP arriving there at 8.30 a.m. 'A' Coy on detail to do entraining duties for 73rd Bde Group. Battn rested for remainder of the day. 13st were under canvas.	
	W.5.		Fine. 'A' Coy reported 13st at 10 a.m. Battalion on march to ROCQUIGNY leaving at 12.25 p.m. & arriving at 5-3.5 p.m. Battn was billeted in Nissen huts.	
ROCQUIGNY	Th.6.		Showery. Parade under Company arrangements. Lt. N.S. Offord and 18 Other ranks proceeded on loan to H.R.S. Johnson advanced from base. 2/Lt. Fowden returned from weapons course.	
	F.7.		Rain. Training under Company arrangement. Rifle range used by all Companies Routine practice for officers.	

2353 Wt. W2544/1454 700,000 5/15 D. D. & L. A.D.S.S./Forms/C. 2118.

Army Form C. 2118.

WAR DIARY
or
INTELLIGENCE SUMMARY.
(Erase heading not required.)

Instructions regarding War Diaries and Intelligence Summaries are contained in F. S. Regs., Part II. and the Staff Manual respectively. Title pages will be prepared in manuscript.

Place	Date Dec.	Hour	Summary of Events and Information	Remarks and references to Appendices
ROCQUIGNY	S. 8.		Showery. Companies were at disposal of Coy. Commanders. Specialist classes held during the morning. 13th was warned to be in readiness to move at 2 hrs notice. 13th Field Ambulance ?	
	Sun 9		Heavy rain. Church parade in C.S.E. Y.M.C.A. 13th marched to MONMOUTH CAMP - BAPAUME. arriving at 3 p.m. 75th Bde being in Divisional Reserve in relief of 32nd Division.	
MONMOUTH CAMP BAPAUME	M. 10.		Fine. The whole of the day devoted to making camp habitable. 13th under command of Major E.R.S. Prior M.C. left B? today to assume Command of II B? Cheshire Regt.	
	T. 11.		Fine frosty. Inspection of camp by Commanding Officer. Major A. Reade M.C. assumed order of 2nd in Command. Companies carried out range practices and Bayonet fighting. Capt. Manning and 16 other ranks proceeded on leave.	
	W. 12.		Fine frosty. Bayonet fighting and short range practices carried out during morning. Specialists in due course given. 2/Lt. J.E.D. Hill, & 2/Lt. P.J. Charlton & 2/Lt. A.J. Whin proceeded to join 1/6 19th South Lancs Regt. Capt. E.G.R. Strutton returned from leave.	
	Th. 13.		Fine frosty. Training as yesterday. Baths allotted 1012 - 13th football team against 3rd C.C.S. 2 - 0.	

Army Form C. 2118.

WAR DIARY
or
INTELLIGENCE SUMMARY.
(Erase heading not required.)

Place	Date Dec.	Hour	Summary of Events and Information	Remarks and references to Appendices
MONMOUTH CAMP BAPAUME	F. 14		Fine frosty. Short Battalion Parade. Men went on musketry course. Special attention being given to 2nd in Command & Platoon & other ranks. Football N.C.Os v Subaltern Officers 3-0.	
	Sat. 15		Fine. Range practice physical training and bayonet fighting during morning. Coy arrangement at 2 p.m. Batt moved to No 5 Camp FAVREUIL arriving at 3-15 p.m.	
No 5 CAMP FAVREUIL.	Sun. 16		Fine. C of E. Service 11 a.m. taken by Commanding Officer. R.C. Parade at 11 a.m. Inter-platoon football competition commenced in the afternoon. 2/Lt R.H. Price returned from 1st Army Infantry School. 2/Lt Green & six other ranks arrived from leave. 2/Lt E. Foulkes & 14 other ranks proceeded on leave.	
	M. 17		Snow. C Coy detailed for work at Durie Mill. Gen. Remainder of Bn employed in making bomb proof tranvision round huts. 2/Lt B.M. Green transferred to 1/5 South Lancs Regt. Inter platoon competition continued during afternoon.	
	T. 18		Frost. Snow. Work continued as yesterday. Recreation also as yesterday. Batt attended to TB=	
	W. 19		Fine. Training under Coy arrangement. During afternoon tactical exercises for Junior officers. Senior officers reconnoitred trenches to be taken over turn off/Brig. at dusk.	
	Th. 20		Frost. Training as yesterday. Junior officers reconnoitred trenches. Night movement of India supplies for carrying cable from PARIS to	

Army Form C. 2118.

WAR DIARY
or
INTELLIGENCE SUMMARY
(Erase heading not required.)

Instructions regarding War Diaries and Intelligence Summaries are contained in F. S. Regs., Part II. and the Staff Manual respectively. Title Pages will be prepared in manuscript.

Place	Date	Hour	Summary of Events and Information	Remarks and references to Appendices
No 5. CAMP FAVREUIL	F. 21 Dec		Front. 13th relieved 1st Batt Cheshire Regt. in front line trenches & support & reserve LAGNICOURT. Right company marched at 2.15 p.m. Relief completed by 6.45 p.m. 2/Lt W.G. Shuttle resigned from comp. wat 2/Lt R.H. Price & 10 other ranks proceeded on leave.	
LAGNICOURT SECTOR	Sat. 22		Front & Snow. Intermittent shelling during day. All available men employed during night wiring in front of line of outposts. Strong patrol 2/Lt Grew & 14 other ranks patrolled for two hours Cavalerie. 1 other rank killed	
	Sun. 23		Hard frost. Work of deepening & widening our trench on extreme left of sector commence at Wanxy also continued. Patrols some strength as yesterday located Enemy outpost strong by kild. 2/Lt HSE Capper & 9 other ranks returned from leave.	
	M. 24		Hard frost. Work continued as yesterday. During reminder condid were inside company relief took place between supports & front line companies at 4p.m. Strong patrol during night (Officers & other ranks) Cavalerie - 1 other rank wounded.	
	T. 25		Frost. Intermittent shelling during day. Work continued as on previous days. Strong patrol sent out at 4 a.m. Nothing of importance to report on return. 2/Lt T.H. Parker returned from 12th Corps Infantry School. 2/Lt Jn Patterson proceeded to England for duty with Tanks Corps.	

WAR DIARY or INTELLIGENCE SUMMARY

Army Form C. 2118.

Place	Date	Hour	Summary of Events and Information	Remarks and references to Appendices
LAMICOURT SECTOR	Dec. W. 26		Frost & snow. Hostile shelling increased. Work as on previous day. Patrols sent out at 12-30 a.m. were subjected to cross fire from two enemy outposts which were located.	
	Th. 27		Hard frost. B~n~ was relieved in front line trenches by XI/3~rd~ Cheshire Regt. Relief commenced at 4 p.m. & was complete by 5-30 p.m. The IV~th~ Coy. Commander made a tour of front line trenches before returning. 2/Lt C O'M. Dowd & 2/Lt Randles remained on leave.	
	Fri. 28		Bliggard. All available men working under R.E. Sweeping new front line trench and also HOBART AVENUE & BOLTON TRENCH. 2/Lt. O.S. Huthey wounded (S.I.) Lt. P.C.C. Forward proceeded to 141 Field Ambulance. Princess Capt. H.L. Ross proceeded to attend 3~rd~ Army Infantry Course.	
	Sat. 29		Frost. Work continued as on previous day. Hostile shelling more severe during night.	
	Sun. 30~th~		Slight snow. Shelling fairly active during day. Commenced supply of mail from LEEDS RESERVE to BOLTON AVENUE. This was continued as on previous day. Commenced ration up mule line L'HINDRELLE VALLEY.	
	M. 31~st~		Slight thaw, cost nearer during day. Frost & snow during night. Work continued as yesterday. Intermittent shelling during day. Very quiet during night.	

J.S. Munro
Commdg. 8th Bn. South Lancs. Regt.

Army Form C. 2118.

WAR DIARY
or
INTELLIGENCE SUMMARY.
(Erase heading not required.)

8 S Lancs Vol 26

Instructions regarding War Diaries and Intelligence Summaries are contained in F. S. Regs., Part II. and the Staff Manual respectively. Title pages will be prepared in manuscript.

Place	Date	Hour	Summary of Events and Information	Remarks and references to Appendices
LAGNICOURT LEFT SUB-SECTOR.	Jany 1918. T.1		Very cold. Slight fall of snow. Enemy activity normal. 7th Sanford & 2 other ranks proceeded for leave. 2/Lt Shaw, 2/Lt Munson & 2/Lt Mackay & 9 men to various to 4th Corps School.	
	W.2		Frost continues. Battalion were relieved in Brigade Support by 10th Rifle Bde. Eastern Regt. and on relief marched to Dien! Pierre. Relief completed by 10.30 p.m.	
FAVREUIL	Th.3		Weather cold. Coy M.G.'s were employed in conjunction with platoons. Work of providing parties to provide working parties for Canadian corps at O.S. for Sgt. Bay was attached to 59th Squadron R.F.E.	
	F.4		Frost still continues. All the day spent as not Coys. on arrival on 2nd line deposition by Major Deverell. 2/Lt John R.F.E. flying instruction and tactical exercises of MG. in pigeon service & carrier pigeon.	
	Sat.5		Still very cold. All men provided with good warm clothes & warm food. R.R.1. Junk. 7th Sergeants present at dinner.	
	S.6		Morning muster Church parade. In all denominations. Also general for all employment. Services & preparation conference.	
	M.7		Regt. show during day - pure again at night. Training carried on in Coy. arrangements. 7th O.R. Set Copt. joined as 2/ADEPT to attend 3day Gas Course.	
	T.8		Heavy show during day. 8 OR Coy. employed on work and forming A&C Coys. training shaping parties.	

28 A

Army Form C. 2118.

WAR DIARY
or
INTELLIGENCE SUMMARY.
(Erase heading not required.)

Instructions regarding War Diaries and Intelligence Summaries are contained in F. S. Regs., Part II. and the Staff Manual respectively. Title pages will be prepared in manuscript.

Place	Date Jan.	Hour	Summary of Events and Information	Remarks and references to Appendices
FAVREUIL	W. 9		Still raining. All companies on the Rifle ranges carrying out range practises. Officers taken on individual exercises	
	Th. 10		Heavy rain during day. Ranges carried out under company arrangements. B. Machine Gun paraded in town.	
	F. 11		Route during night of most during day. All companies working as own line of LAGNICOURT SECTOR.	
	Sat. 12		Five sporty all companies at disposal of G.O.C. (commander in position) in pulling out platoon positions during afternoon	
	S. 13		The whole Bn. worked on the construction of the VAULX - MORCHIES LINE. The Battalion arrived at England sick.	
	M. 14		The Bn. relieved the 10th Bn. Cheshire Regt. (LEFT SUB SECTOR) in the front line. Relief complete at 8 p.m.	
LAGNICOURT LEFT SUB-SECTOR.	T. 15		Heavy shew & rain. Enemy quiet. Below normal. Patrols available enemy were during night but had nothing of note to report. The Battn. admitted to hospital sick.	
	W. 16		Rain. Our General made a tour of front line trenches. All working parties of trenches commenced. The enemy is reported three trench mortar bombardment.	
	Th. 17		Slight rain. Commanders of the front line par. out all except during hours of stand-down. All available labour utilised in wiring communication sets & Valley prominent on them	

A5834 Wt. W4973/M687 750,000 8/16 D.D. & L. Ltd. Forms/C.2118/13.

Army Form C. 2118.

WAR DIARY
or
INTELLIGENCE SUMMARY.
(Erase heading not required.)

Place	Date	Hour	Summary of Events and Information	Remarks and references to Appendices
LAGNICOURT LEFT SUB-SECTOR.	F. 18.		Slight enemy activity about normal except in increased activity and movement about LAGNICOURT mostly of working parties. Communication trench adversely swept by enemy at moment par parts manned by machine guns now in HARPONVILLE VALLEY.	
	SAT. 19		Patrols during night encountered enemy still front line by means of newer conditions. 2 other ranks wounded. 5th R.B. Lieutenants admitted to hospital.	
	S. 20.		Our enemy activity of gun and trench mortar. 137 returned in front line trenches by 11th Bn 13th Bde Infantry. Reps. & M.G. into BRIGADE RESERVE at VAULX. Relief complete by 7.7pm. 7th Battalion proceeded on leave.	
VAULX.	M. 21.		Whole of Battalion employed on working parties under R.E./o.	
	T. 22.		Battalion employed under R.E./o in continuation of work yesterday. Reinforcements - 5 O.R.b. reported for duty.	
	W. 23.	Rain.	Work continued as on previous day. Reinforcements 4 O.Rb. reported for duty.	
	Th. 24.	Misty.	Works under R.E.b continued.	
	F. 25.		Works under R.E./o. 15 day men and other returned from Corps School. Casualties Lt. Hollin North wounded. 3 O.R.b. killed 14 wounded. with many 13 worked.	

O.C. W.F. BRYDEN M.C. Battalion in Com.

Army Form C. 2118.

WAR DIARY
or
INTELLIGENCE SUMMARY.
(Erase heading not required.)

Instructions regarding War Diaries and Intelligence Summaries are contained in F. S. Regs., Part II. and the Staff Manual respectively. Title pages will be prepared in manuscript.

Place	Date	Hour	Summary of Events and Information	Remarks and references to Appendices
VAULX.	S.26.		Whole Battalion working in VAULX-MORCHIES line. Bath relieves in Bde. reserve by 10th Yorkshire Regt. moved into Divisional Reserve at FAVREUIL. Relief complete by 3.30 p.m.	
FAVREUIL	Sun 27.		Church Parades for all denominations. Remainder of day devoted to general cleaning up. Parties of 2 N.C.O's & 13 men worked on Div. HQ.s. Remainder of	
	M.28.		Two hours close order drill under Company arrangements. Remainder of day spent in protection of huts against air raids. Sandbags built around huts, tents.	
	T.29. Rain (slight)		Baths at BAPAUME (180 men) 8 Officers and 416 men working on NRF communication trench under R.E's and proceeded by light railway as far as NOREUIL. Major A. REANE M.C. proceeded to 10th Yorkshire Regt. and in Command	
	W.30.		Baths at BAPAUME (180 men) Few bombs were dropped on Thursday. Several bombs were dropped but no damage done. Forward communication trench continued. FAVREUIL between 10.30 pm & 12.30 am	
	Th.31.		Battalion returned from parade for G.O.C.'s inspection	Lt. Col. J.R.

Lt. Col.
Commdg. 8th (Service) Battn.

1/2/07

This document
.... WO 95/2250 ....

Has been borrowed by
.... Emily ....

For
....
....

Please leave this note on the
document when you have finished

Thank You

For the attention of staff

Return this document
to..... Photo est ....

Note: After this note
all refer to 2nd Battalion
S Lancs — another folder in
this box

www.ingramcontent.com/pod-product-compliance
Lightning Source LLC
Chambersburg PA
CBHW081432160426
43193CB00013B/2258